TACKLING FUNDAMENTALS AND TECHNIQUES

KEVIN BULLIS
TOM JOURNELL

ISBN: 1-58518-318-0

Library of Congress Catalog Card Number: 00-106283

Cover Design and Page Layout: Paul W. Lewis

Coaches Choice
P.O. Box 1828
Monterey, CA 93942
www.coacheschoiceweb.com

DEDICATION

To my wife, Kathy, and our two beautiful sons, Jack and Joe, thank you for your love and support. To my parents, Jerry and Lucille, thank you for your support in pursuing my dreams.

__Kevin Bullis

This book is dedicated to my wife, Betsy, and to my son, Mack. You are the stabilizing forces in my life. I also want to thank my parents and grandparents. They instilled a burning desire for results and success in me for which I can be eternally grateful.

__Tom Journell

ACKNOWLEDGEMENTS

The authors are very grateful to John O'Grady, head football coach at the University of Wisconsin – River Falls, who has given us the support and leadership to develop our knowledge and skills as coaches. John is a student of the game, and he reinforces that attribute in us.

The authors give a special acknowledgment to Bob Fello, defensive line coach at Kansas State University, who has been an excellent source for football information over the past nine years. He taught us the importance of emphasizing all the aspects of tackling.

CONTENTS

The fabric of football is blocking and tackling. Regardless of the scheme run on defense, tackling determines the success of the defense and the team. In the 1993 season we missed 142 tackles. This equates to 14.2 per game. Our team finished 6-4. In the off-season we challenged ourselves to find a better way to teach tackling. In 1994 we cut our missed tackle numbers in half. Ever since, we have been below 80 missed tackles for the year. Analysis of game-tape statistics demonstrates that typically when we miss over eight tackles in a game, more often then not, we lost.

Since we improved the teaching of tackling, we have been to the Division III playoffs twice; we have won the conference championship and have been conference runners up four times. In addition, we have led the conference in total defense three times. In other words, since refining our teaching of tackling, our defense and team have made dramatic improvements.

When we were approached to publish a book and video series, the first topic we thought of was tackling. When we perused the literature, we were amazed at the lack of published information on tackling. We are excited to share how we teach tackling and all of the position specific tackling drills. For instructional purposes, this book is broken down into three sections:

➠ **TACKLE PROGRESSION:** How we teach tackling in a three-phase progression.

➠ **POSITION SPECIFIC TACKLING DRILLS:** This book can be a resource for position coaches. We have broken down specific tackling drills into defensive line, linebacker and defensive back positions.

➠ **PURSUIT AND TAKEAWAYS:** You can not be a great tackling team without being a great pursuit and takeaway team. We consider tackling, pursuit and takeaways all in the same breath. For example, if your corner misses an open-field tackle, your defensive team's pursuit better be close to compensate for the corner's mistake.

PHOTO 1.1

PHOTO 1.2

Regardless of position, we believe in tackling everyday. In addition, we put a high premium on coaching tackling, pursuit and taking the ball away in every individual, group and team period. We assign a young, ambitious coach on our staff to be the pursuit and takeaway coach. On every snap in every group and team period, this coach flies around screaming "run to the ball, get it out, take it away".

Filming tackling drills is paramount. We film all tackling drills for evaluation and for teaching. Players need to see proper tackling techniques as well as incorrect tackling technique.

SAFETY AND PROPER CONTACT AREAS

Before getting started with the fundamentals of tackling, we would like to cover the proper body position and contact points when executing a safe tackle. We like to use the phrase "the 4 ups of tackling": head up, eyes up, chest up and arms up. **Photo 1.1** shows a tackler in the proper contact position. When performing a proper tackle, the tackler's hips, knees and ankles are in a bent position (i.e. squat stance), his chest is out, his shoulder blades are together, and his head is up. **Photo 1.2** illustrates an improper tackling position. This position is very weak. Note the tackler's legs are straight, and his head is down. The player is overextended and exposing his head. There can be no force generated from this stance. Contact should be made with the chest and the anterior, rounded part of the shoulder pads. We do not talk to our players about helmet contact, other than the fact that it should not be done.

CHAPTER I

TACKLE PROGRESSION

What did we change in 1994 when we decided that we needed to improve our tackling? We implemented a series of base tackling drills called Tackle Progression or circuit tackling. This approach is the keystone of how we teach tackling. The advantages of the circuit are:

➡ It involves a high number of repetitions without high-speed impacts. Therefore, it is a relatively safe way to get hundreds of reps

➡ It can be implemented without pads.

➡ Players know what to do with their arms when tackling.

➡ A system featuring high reps with low impact allows everyone to experience success; this success subsequently increases confidence.

➡ Players who have initially been shy of contact have learned to accept contact and have turned out to be solid tacklers. Players get to know and feel proper contact points.

➡ On contact, players know what to do with their feet.

Players work in pairs. Individuals in each pair should be relatively the same size and athletic ability. We emphasize tempo and safety tips in each drill so that players understand the points of emphasis and the tempo of each drill.

There are three phases to the Progression. In order to teach the progression of tackling, we simultaneously teach each drill to the entire defense and the players on special teams the first practice. The next practice, we break up the defense into three groups and rotate the groups through the circuit. During two-a-days, we perform the circuit everyday. During the season, we conduct the circuit once per week, although each position coach performs position-specific tackling drills every practice. In fact, we tackle the day before games — a practice that is an extension of our firm belief that it is important to tackle everyday.

At the beginning of the season, we allocate 15 - 20 minutes for the Circuit. In addition, we allow extra time for instruction and compromise repetitions. Once the players know the Progression, we allocate three minutes per station or 10 minutes for the Progression. At the end of each phase, the coach in charge of his station will huddle with the players at that station. The players then rotate clockwise and hustle to the next station.

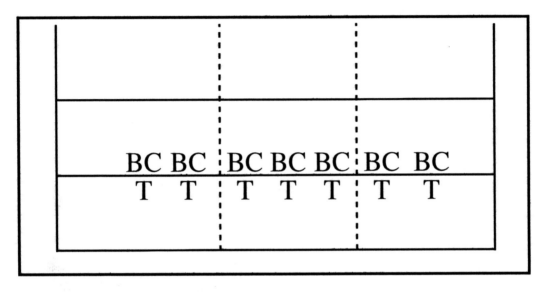

Diagram 1.1
Organization of the tackling progression:
one knee down, wrap with arms and hands.

Sometimes during the season, there is a tendency for players and coaches to just "go through the motions" during the Progression. Therefore, it is essential that coaches demand hustle and strict adherence to proper tackling technique. Coaches must constantly use instructional language during the Circuit, just like during the first week of practice. We sometimes start practice with the Progression just to set the tone of practice.

THE PROGRESSION/CIRCUIT

Phase One: One Knee Down, Wrap Up

This drill is the first one we teach in the Progression. This is an UPPER BODY DRILL ONLY! The lower body cannot come into play. Warning: If the tackler uses his lower body, the ball carrier may be bent backward and might be injured. We are emphasizing arm angles and grabbing cloth in this phase. We like this drill to be the first in the Progression since it can be controlled. The desired tempo of the drill is 3/4 speed, using the upper body only.

➠ **Diagram 1.1** shows the set-up of the drill. Players are paired up on a line, with one yard between pairs. A tackler's side and a ball carrier's side should be designated.

➠ **Photo 1.1** demonstrates the starting position of the players in this drill. Both players are down on the same knee (i.e., tackler is on his right knee, and the ball carrier is on his right knee). The players' hips and chests are close together. The down knee for each individual should be close to each other. The up knee should be next to his partner's hip. The down knee will determine the side of the shoulder contact. In other words, if the right knee is down, the tackler will make a right-shoulder hit. In addition, the helmet should be aligned to the left of the ball carrier.

➠ The head and chest are up. We stress that the tackler should be lower than the ball carrier. Players should be reminded not to use their lower body! At the coach's "READY" command, the tackler extends his arms back as far as possible, keeping his elbows at 90 degrees. His elbows should remain at 90 degrees so as to create a shorter lever and thus faster arms on the tackle. The analogy we use to describe this concept is boxing. When a boxer throws an uppercut, the elbow position is 90 degrees. If the boxer threw this punch with a straight arm, the punch would not have force and would be too slow.

➠ **Photo 1.2** exhibits one of the most common mistakes in tackling — straight arms during the wrap. It is one of the easiest factors to see when conducting all phases of the Progression. We feel paying special detail to the uppercuts throughout the Progression will dramatically improve tackling.

Photo 1.1

Photo 1.2

➠ **Photo 1.3** illustrates the drill after the "HIT" command has been made by the coach. The emphasis here should be on the wrap. We want to club the arms upward and grab cloth as high as possible on the back of the ball carrier's jersey. When this is accomplished, the head is up, the chest is up and the eyes are up. When the tackler's arms are moved in the vertical plane, it is easier for his hips to be incorporated. If a tackler wraps his arms around the ball carrier in the horizontal plane, his hips have a tougher time coming through, his body becomes overextended, and the top of his head is exposed.

➠ Grabbing cloth. After each "HIT" command, the tackler must forcefully grab cloth until the "READY" command of the next repetition. In between each command, coaches must check the grip of the tackler and try to rip the tackler's hands away. The concept of no hidden yardage should be reinforced. The tackler should not let go until told to do so by the coach.

➠ After 10 repetitions for each shoulder, the tacklers should be switched. After both individuals have executed one side, the tacklers should switch knees and execute 10 repetitions each with the other shoulder.

Photo 1.3

➡ **Photo 1.4** illustrates how our players train their forearm muscles year round. Grip strength is one area that is often overlooked in the weight room. On every power rack, squat rack, or 5th-quarter station, we tape towels or old jerseys, and our players grab them and do as many pull ups as they can. We call these exercises towel pull-ups. Once a player is relatively exhausted, we then challenge him to hang on as long as possible. This practice reinforces the idea of finishing the tackle and never letting go of the ball carrier. We require our players to perform towel pull-ups twice per week throughout the year.

This drill is an effective method for achieving maximum repetitions in a short period of time with low impact. Through this drill, players understand and feel proper contact. We really believe this drill trains/conditions players to be more accepting of contact.

To summarize, the three primary commands by the coach during this phase are:

➡ "READY" — the arms of the tackler are ripped back, and his elbows are at 90 degrees

➡ "HIT" — the arms and hands of the tackler shoot through the ball carrier

➡ "GRAB CLOTH" — the tackler clubs his arms up and grabs cloth as high as possible on the back of the ball carrier's jersey. The coach should try to peel off the tackler's hands in order to test both his grip strength and his resolve to continue holding on. Tacklers continue to grab cloth until the next "READY" command.

Phase Two: Down on Both Knees, Hip Explosion and Wrap

This drill emphasizes hips and arms together. The tempo of this drill is full speed. As with the first phase of the Progression, this drill is close quartered. This drill is designed to teach hitting with proper pad level. Players feel how and where to make contact. It should be emphasized that a tackler should make contact with his chest and the front, rounded portion of his shoulder pad. This drill is tailored for this contact (i.e., the fit position discussed in the first chapter).

Photo 1.4

Photo 1.5

Photo 1.6

➡ The players should be paired up on a line. A tackling side and a ball-carrying side should be designated. The tackler should be down on both knees, while the ball carrier should be standing about a foot away. The ball carrier should be offset **(Photo 1.5 back view)** so the tackler is making contact with his shoulder and chest. Tacklers should sit on their heels and curl their toes under to get into a proper coiled position.

➡ **Photo 1.6** displays the position of the tackler on the "READY" command. As in phase one, the tackler's elbows are cocked at 90 degrees and ripped back. Both his head and chest are up.

➡ **Photo 1.7** shows the "HIT" phase of the drill. This drill incorporates the "HIT" part of phase one with the addition of use of the tackler's hips. The tackler uncoils his body and explodes with his arms and hips working together. As mentioned previously, it is easier for the tackler's arms and hips to work together since they are working in the same vertical plane. Furthermore, clubbing the arms upward keeps the tackler's chest and head upright. If his arms are wrapping around in the horizontal or transverse plane as seen in **Photo 1.8**, his hips become locked, his body becomes overextended, and the top of his head is exposed. The coach should emphasize the importance of the tackler extending his toes and plantar flexing his ankle joint. The tackler should grab cloth high on the back of the ball carrier's shoulder pads and hold until the "READY" command. As in phase one, coaches should check the grip of the tackler.

➡ After five repetitions with one shoulder, the ball carrier should offset the other side and execute five repetitions with the other shoulder. The tacklers should then be switched.

➡ Injury prevention. While some coaches believe that the tackler should have a bowed or negative arch in his back on the "HIT" phase **(Photo 1.9),** we believe that the tackler's back should be straight (i.e., not arched) on and through contact. We teach this concept similar to how we teach a squat lift or a clean lift. If players are arching their backs, a lower back injury could occur. While we want the tackler to keep his eyes up, we actually want his eyes to be focused through the ball carrier. We avoid using the phrase "eyes to the sky" because we believe this approach may encourage players to arch their backs.

Photo 1.7

Photo 1.8

Photo 1.9

To summarize, the commands by the coach during this phase are:

➡ "READY" — the arms of the tackler are ripped back and his elbows are at 90 degrees. The tackler should sit on his heels and curl his toes under, ready to uncoil.

➡ "HIT" — the arms, hands and hips of the tackler shoot through the ball carrier. The tackler's hips and arms are connected and travel through the same plane.

➡ "GRAB CLOTH" — the tackler clubs his arms up and grabs cloth as high as possible on the back of the ball carrier's jersey.

Phase Three: *Angle Tackle or Pit Tackle*

ANGLE TACKLE DRILL

➡ We use the angle tackle drill during the acclimatization or non-contact period during 2-a-days. We also use it with the pit tackling drill throughout the year. This drill is the same as the drill described in phase two, except for the addition of the tackler's feet. During this drill, the emphasis is on the tackler's feet. Upon contact, we want the tackler's feet to be active or churning. Because a tackler rarely takes on a ball carrier nose to nose, our emphasis is on angling the drill. This drill is conducted full speed on contact. The tackler should not take the ball carrier to the ground. In other words, this drill is performed "live on the feet."

➡ Players should be paired on a line. A tackling side and a ball-carrying side should be designated. Each group should be a minimum of five yards apart. The players should spread out. With no pads, the tackler and the ball carrier should be an arms length away from each other. With pads on, the tackler and the ball carrier can be up to five yards apart. The tackler and the ball carrier are slightly angled. The coach should instruct the direction of the ball carrier and the tackler.

➡ **Photo 1.10** shows the "READY" command. The tacklers are in a staggered, bent-knee position with their arms ripped back at 90 degrees.

➡ **Photo 1.11** exhibits the "HIT" command. The ball carrier will run about half speed at the same starting angle. The tackler is instructed to "step on the toes" of the ball carrier and explode on the rise through the ball carrier. The emphasis should be for the tackler to run his feet.

Photo 1.10

➠ The helmet of the tackler should go across the ball carrier in order to drive the ball carrier back from where he started. Ideally, the ball carrier should driven back 2-3 yards.

➠ After knocking the ball carrier back, the tackler and the ball carrier should be required to hustle back to the starting position for another repetition.

➠ Initially, the drill involves tackling in the same direction with the same tackler for three repetitions. After which, the tacklers and the ball carriers switch. To save time, the partners can stay on their same side. The ball carrier should be instructed which direction to run and the tackler should be told which shoulder to hit. After each player has executed three tackles with one shoulder, he should rotate to the other shoulder.

➠ This drill is the slowest one in the Circuit and requires the most technical instruction. It is essential that coaches be clear and loud in their instructions. While many repetitions can be accomplished in the first two phases, typically each tackler will execute only about six tackles (three per side) in this phase.

Photo 1.11

PIT TACKLE DRILL

We use the pit tackle drill later in 2-a-days and throughout the season as the third phase of the Circuit or Progression. In this drill the tackler will tackle and drive the ball carrier onto a soft crash pad or high jump pit. This drill is particularly appropriate since the tackler can execute a full-speed tackle without the ball carrier being injured. In addition, this is an effective way to identify the "natural" tacklers, those with great hip explosion. We always video tape this phase the first day we introduce the drill at practice to facilitate the process of identifying the skill level of each player.

➡ **Diagram 1.2** shows the set-up of the drill. The ball carrier aligns in front of the cone. The coach stands three feet in front of the pit so the ball carrier will not be carried over the pit. The tackler faces the ball carrier and the pit, two yards from the ball carrier. To control the drill, a cone is placed at the starting point for the tackler. The tackler rotates to the other side of the pit after executing the tackle. The other side can go once the pit is clear.

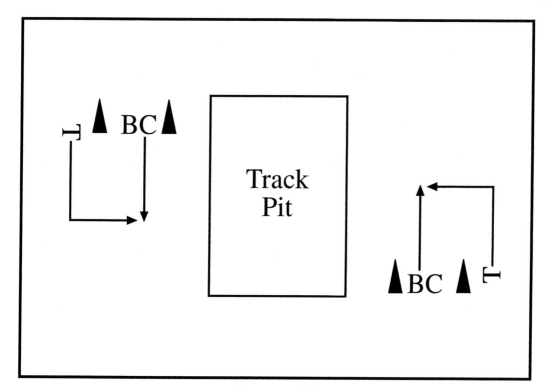

Diagram 1.2
Organization of the pit tackle drill.

➧ **Photo 1.12** demonstrates what occurs on the "READY" command. The ball carrier slowly jogs to the center of the pad. The tackler will execute a lateral shuffle in anticipation of the "HIT" command. The tackler should stay in a low position, taking short, quick shuffle steps.

➧ **Photo 1.13** exhibits what occurs on the "HIT" command. Ideally, the contact point should be in the center of the pit. The coach should coordinate the "HIT" command when the tackler reaches the contact point. On the "HIT" command, the tackler quickly rips his arms back at 90 degrees and then explodes his feet, hips and arms on the tackle. We want the tackler's helmet in front of the ball carrier. The tackler must continue to drive or churn his feet in order to take the ball carrier onto the pit. It is easy to pinpoint the tacklers who need to "run their feet" because these are the individuals who stop their feet on contact.

➧ **Photo 1.14 (behind the pit)** displays the finish of the drill.

➧ The rotation of this drill is relatively simple. The tackler goes to the line of ball carriers, and the ball carrier goes to the line of tacklers. If possible, two to three pits should be used to increase repetitions. Sufficient personnel should staff each pit to ensure the players' safety. Players should be able to get at least six tackles (i.e., three per shoulder).

➧ This drill is a capstone for the Circuit. It represents a synthesis of each phase in the Progression. We again encourage the use of videotape to evaluate players and to use as a teaching tool.

DIAMOND TACKLE DRILL

Another drill we use to cap off the Progression is called the diamond tackle.

➧ **Diagram 1.3** illustrates the set up of this drill. Two cones are placed five yards apart, preferably on lines. The ball carrier aligns across from the tackler on the far cone. The tackler aligns on the other cone next to the coach.

➧ **Photo 1.15** demonstrates what occurs on the "READY" command. On "READY," the ball carrier runs directly at the coach. At the same time, the tackler will execute an angle tackle with his helmet across the ball carrier.

Photo 1.12

Photo 1.13

Photo 1.14

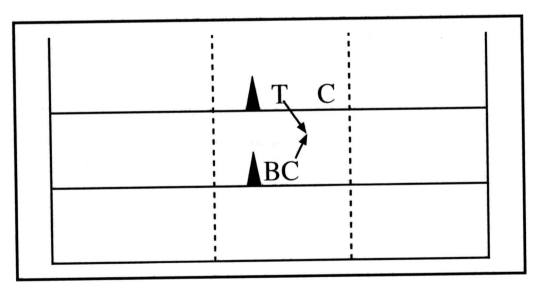

Diagram 1.3
Organization of the diamond tackle drill.

Photo 1.15

Photo 1.16

➡ **Photo 1.16** exhibits what occurs on the "HIT" command. Upon contact, the tackler wants to run his feet and drive the ball carrier back past the line from which he started. The drill does not end until the tackler drives the ball carrier past this point. After each player has executed the tackle, the coach changes sides. In addition, the coach can change the angle of the tackle by standing farther from the tackler.

CHAPTER 2

Defensive Linemen

Defensive linemen seldom find themselves in an open-field tackle situation. However, when it does occur, it is a crucial instance. Probably the most important open-field tackle they will make during a game is a quarterback sack. The concepts of tackling a quarterback in a pass situation are very similar to those involved when a defensive back makes a tackle in the open field. Rarely is a quarterback sack a nice clean form tackle (unless the quarterback does not see the tackler). The following key points apply to situations where the quarterback sees the pass rusher coming:

Pass Rush Lanes

Pass rush lanes are the pass rusher's pursuit angle on the quarterback. In this situation, a pass rusher should adhere to three fundamental guidelines:

➠ Never follow the same color jersey.

➠ Keep the rush as balanced as possible.

➠ Force the ball carrier to your help.

Additional points of emphasis concerning pass rushing responsibilities and techniques include:

➠ Defensive ends (outside pass rushers) should attack a point one yard outside the shoulder of the QB (**DIAGRAM 2.1**). This pathway ensures that the QB will not escape from the pocket. Depending on the ability of the QB and the skills of the defensive ends, the aiming point on the QB can be adjusted.

➠ Defensive tackles (inside pass rushers) should attack the near jersey number of the QB. This action will force the quarterback to the rusher's inside help. The pass rusher typically has more help to the inside. If the defensive tackle pressures the QB to the outside, it will become an unbalanced pass rush, and one defensive end will be on an island (**DIAGRAM 2.2).**

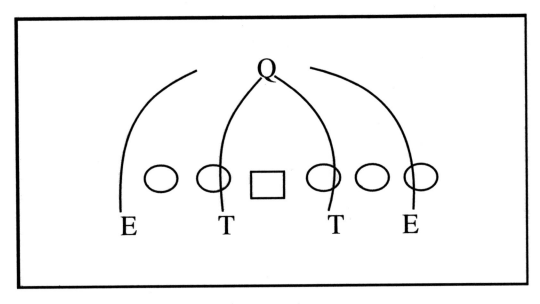

Diagram 2.1
Pass rush aiming points on the quarterback.

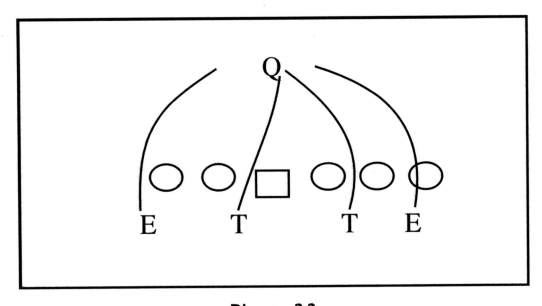

Diagram 2.2
Defensive lineman should stay in their lanes to keep a balanced pass rush.

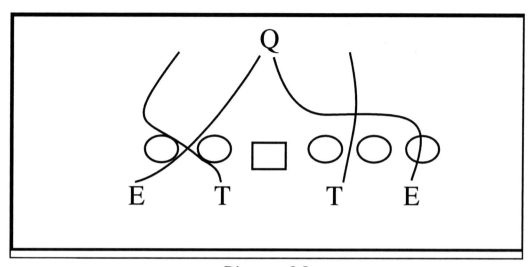

Diagram 2.3
Pass rush responsibilities change with stunts.

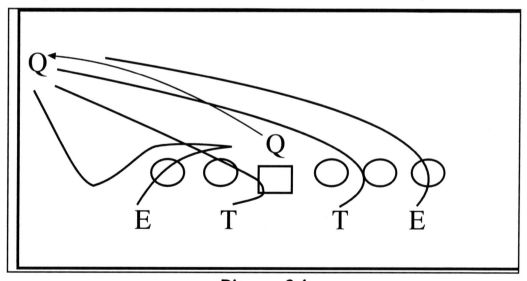

Diagram 2.4
Aiming points should be adjusted to the quarterback.

➡ Because pass rush stunts can change the rusher's lane responsibilities, players must understand the change. When a defensive tackle becomes responsible for an outside pass rush, he should widen his aiming point to two yards outside the QB because typically a defensive tackle is less athletic than a defensive end **(DIAGRAM 2.3)**.

➡ The pass rush lanes adjust to the QB and move when he moves. If the QB is on a play-action boot pass or sprint out, the lanes should adjust to his location.

➡ It is vital that on a play-action boot pass or sprint-out play, that the backside defensive end maintains his backside responsibility. Because great scrambling quarterbacks often like to reverse their field while being pursued, the backside defensive end can lose his outside pass rush positioning if he takes an inappropriate pursuit angle.

➡ The front-side defensive end must play the run on the play-action boot pass. Once he recognizes the QB boot pass, he should take a pursuit angle to cutoff the QB running down the sideline. When the QB pulls up to pass, the defensive end will gain leverage on the quarterback. As such, he can bend his path to the 1 1/2-yard landmark on the quarterback **(DIAGRAM 2.4)**. This drill is very easy to execute.

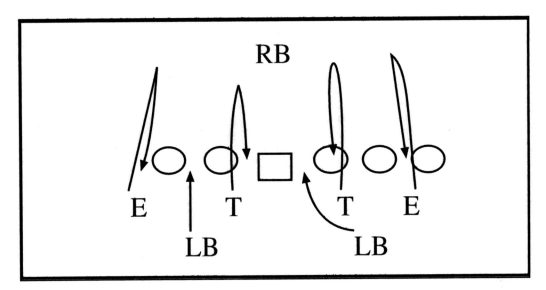

Diagram 2.5
Defensive linemen should retrace their path on draw plays.

⟹ Maintaining a proper pass rush lane is not only crucial on a pass play, but also against a draw play. Linebackers will better understand where they fit into the defensive line and where their help is. Against any draw play, defensive linemen will maintain their pass rush lanes by retracing their steps on recognition of draw. Defensive linemen should plant on their outside foot and retrace facing to the inside. They may need to work a pass-rush move on the retrace. Coaches should reinforce the concept to the defensive lineman that they will have backside angle on the ball carrier, which puts them in a great position to take the ball away. The player set-up in the diagram shown can very easily be transformed into a drill **(DIAGRAM 2.5)**. A coach standing behind the defensive line has the option of signaling the offensive line to block for a pass, draw, or screen. The defensive line must then react accordingly.

Pass Break Up by a Pass Rusher

The only time pass rushers should ever jump or raise their hands to knockdown a pass is against a 3-step drop pass. Jumping or raising hands takes the pass rusher out of the athletic positioning needed to make an open-field tackle on the quarterback. Too often a quarterback will fake the throw to get an oncoming rusher in the air and run around him or get a pass rusher to quit working moves because the defensive player thinks the quarterback is going to throw. Pass rushers should have their eyes on the pass protector. If defensive linemen want to defeat the pass protector, they should have their eyes concentrating on them.

How Does the Opponent's Quarterback React to Pressure?

Knowing how an opponent's QB will react to pressure will give pass-rushers a better idea what angle to leverage the quarterback and will give a team's defensive coordinator a better idea of what stunts and blitzes to call. Some quarterbacks will react to pressure by flushing out the backside of the pocket, while others will have a tendency to step up into the pocket. Defensive ends can tighten their pass rush lane landmark on the quarterback that steps up and loosen their mark on the quarterback that flushes out the backside of the pocket.

Related Drills

QUARTERBACK SACK DRILL
The primary purpose of this drill is to give a defensive lineman an opportunity to work on his skills and techniques in an one-on-one open-field tackle position against a quarterback. We conduct this drill at least once a week. We film this drill so we can use it as a learning tool.

➠ A speed-type player is positioned in a 5x10-yard box in the opposite corner of the pass rusher to simulate being the quarterback. The quarterback cannot leave the 5x10 box but will do everything he can to not get tackled **(DIAGRAM 2.6)**.

➠ On the snap of a football, the pass rusher works a pass-rush move against a pass protector. The pass protector should allow the pass rusher to successfully execute his move by not giving too much resistance.

➠ It is vital that the pass rusher executes a crisp pass-rush move to lessen the opportunity for him developing bad habits.

➠ The pass rusher should leverage the quarterback with the same leverage point he would use in his pass-rush lanes. The defender should force the quarterback to inside help.

➠ While keeping leverage on the quarterback, the pass rusher should continue to close rapidly on the quarterback without lunging or being out of control. He should close with short quick steps. (Refer to the discussion on open-field tackling for additional information.)

➠ The pass rusher should stay in the box until he can get both hands locked on the quarterback. No need exists to take the drill quarterback to ground because the toughest skill and the one that typically needs the most practice is for the defender to get his hands on the quarterback.

QUARTERBACK BACKSIDE HIT DRILL

The primary purpose of this drill is to reinforce the proper technique for tackling the quarterback who does not see the pass rusher coming. This drill should be performed a minimum of once every two weeks.

➠ The quarterback is at a depth of seven yards from the line of scrimmage **(DIAGRAM 2.7)**.

➠ On the snap of the football, the pass rusher makes a pass-rush move on a pass protector. The pass protector lets the pass rusher successfully execute his move by not giving too much resistance. Players should be reminded that this exercise is a tackling drill, not a pass-rush technique drill.

➠ It is vital, however, that the pass rusher executes a crisp pass-rush move to lessen the opportunity for developing bad habits.

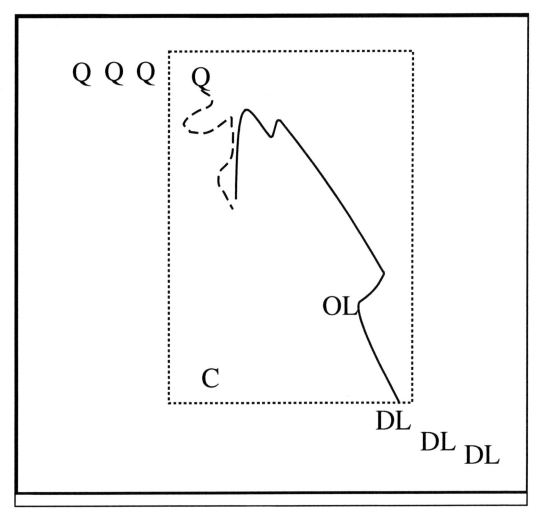

Diagram 2.6
The quarterback sack drill puts the player in an open-field tackle situation.

➡ It is important that the pass rusher accelerates to the quarterback after defeating the pass protector's block.

➡ On impact with the quarterback, the pass rusher should secure the tackle with his arm nearest to the line of scrimmage. Prior to contact, the tackler should let up slightly and not take the quarterback to the ground in the drill. The pass rusher's other arm should spike at the football to cause a fumble.

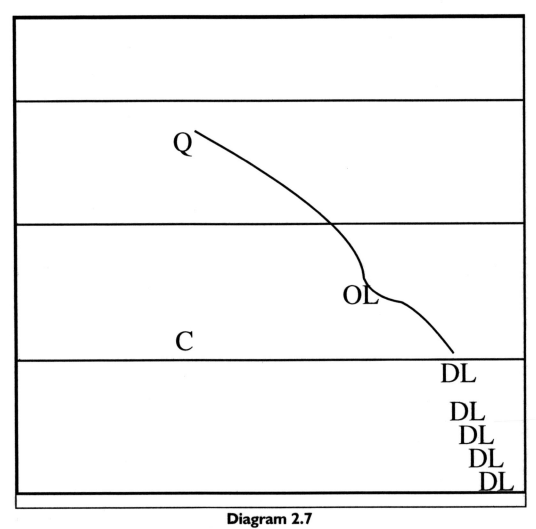

Diagram 2.7
The backside hit drill reinforces getting the ball on a sack.

CHAPTER 3

LINEBACKERS

Depending on the offensive play, a linebacker may find himself in one of several situations, including open-field tackling when blitzing a throwing quarterback, tackling a receiver who has made a reception, tackling a ball carrier on the perimeter, and close-order tackling situations, such as an interior-run play.

GOAL LINE TACKLE DRILL
This drill is designed to develop the ability of the defender to keep his hips between the end zone and the ball carrier.

➠ This drill is conducted at a full or 2/3 speed. To lessen the risk for injury, the tackler should not grab the ball carrier's ankles on a tackle It is a great drill to help determine which players would be effective in heavy-contact positions. Many coaches have reservations about live tackling drills in practice because of fear of injury. We have been doing this drill for over ten years and have never had a player get injured while performing it. Because this drill takes place in a small space and in close order, less opportunity exists for players to get into an injury situation. Another factor that can help to diminish the likelihood of an injury occurring during this drill is for the coach to use a quick whistle.

➠ The players are split into two groups. One side acts as the ball carriers, while the other side serves as the tacklers.

➠ Three large agility bags (1'x3'x6"-10") or blocking dummies are placed parallel to each other, one-yard distance away from each other. The bags are set perpendicular to a line on the field (i.e., the goal line), **(DIAGRAM 3.1)**.

➠ The tacklers are lined up in single file at the end of the middle bag nearest the goal line, and the ball carriers are aligned opposite them.

➠ The ball carrier keeps the ball in his hands while touching the agility bag with the ball. The ball carrier runs to either the left or right alley any time after the coach says "ready." The ball carrier should not give any fakes. At all times during the drill, the ball carrier should remain in a safe running position.

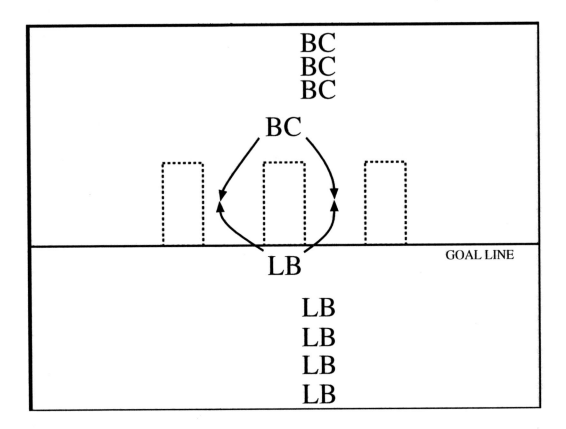

Diagram 3.1
The goal line tackle drill puts a player in a close-order tackle.

➟ When the tackler stops the ball carrier from crossing the end-zone line, the drill is over. This drill can get very competitive, especially if the players are split into two teams.

Key Coaching Points
Frequently, tacklers give up hidden yardage after making contact with the ball carrier. In a close-order situation, giving up hidden yardage can be the result of several factors, including the tackler turning his hips, not keeping his hips in proper positioning, etc. A list of the key coaching points on proper tackling technique includes the following:

A tackler should...

➠ Focus his eyes through the top of the ball carrier's thigh pads.

➠ Make a pad-under-pad hit on the ball carrier. Hitting with leverage can help overcome a lot of tackling mistakes.

➠ Cock and his shoot hands up on contact. This action will result in the tackler's hips getting involved in the hit. Players should be reminded that their hips are the most powerful part of the human body. As such, once the hips are involved, less chance exists for hidden yardage.

➠ Squeeze cloth with his hands to finish the hit.

➠ Drive his feet through on contact and push the ball carrier back where he started.

➠ Get his helmet across the ball carrier's sternum to ensure his tackle does not turn into an arm tackle.

EYE OPENER DRILL

The primary purpose of this drill is to help the inside linebacker develop the abiltiy to maintain an inside/out relationship on the ball carrier **(DIAGRAM 3.2)**. By maintaining inside leverage and eliminating the ball carrier from cutting back, the ball carrier will be forced to the outside run-support defenders.

➠ This drill is conducted at full speed, with the initial hit being live. The defender, however, should not take the ball carrier to the ground. Because this drill is not a close order exercise, a higher potential exists for a player being injured if the drill is not tightly controlled by the coach. The coach should use a quick whistle to limit any opportunity for injury.

➠ Four to five large agility or blocking dummies are set up, parallel and one-yard distance away from each other **(DIAGRAM 3.3)**.

The ball carrier and the tackler are positioned five yards apart facing each other. After the coach signals "READY", the ball carrier has the option of running through any of the alleys made by the agility bags. At the coach's discretion, the ball carrier can employ fakes.

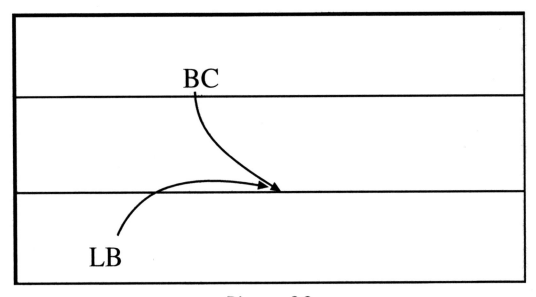

Diagram 3.2
The linebacker should maintain inside leverage on the ball carrier.

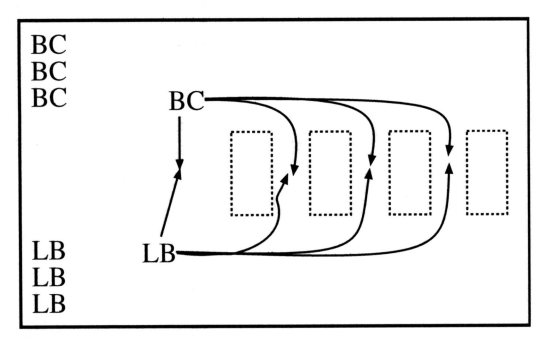

Diagram 3.3
The eye opener drill makes the linebacker keep inside leverage.

Key Coaching Points

To take away the cutback from the ball carrier, the tackler must let the ball carrier lead him. If the tackler gets even with the ball carrier, an opportunity exists for the ball carrier to cut back. The tackler should assume the ball carrier is going to cut back and take an angle of pursuit that will eliminate any cutback possibility. Among the points that should be stressed to each player are the following:

➡ Close on the ball carrier with controlled speed.

➡ Keep his toes pointed towards the line of scrimmage so he has a good power base to make the tackle and can limit the opportunity for hidden yardage. Do not stop his feet.

➡ Focus his eyes through the top of the ball carrier's thigh pads.

➡ Make a pad-under-pad hit on the ball carrier. Hitting with leverage can help minimize the impact of a lot of tackling mistakes.

➡ Cock and shoot his hands up on contact. This action will cause the tackler's hips to get involved in the hit. Players should be reminded that their the hips are the most powerful part of the human body. Once their hips are involved in the tackle, minimal chance exists for hidden yardage.

➡ Squeeze cloth with his hands to finish the hit.

➡ Drive his feet through on contact and push the ball carrier back where he started.

➡ Get his helmet across the ball to ensure his tackle does not turn into an arm tackle.

SHOWDOWN DRILL

This drill is designed to enable a linebacker to develop his open-field tackle skills in a setting near the sideline. Several key concepts exist for making tackle in an open field setting.

➡ The defender should keep inside leverage on the ball carrier. Inside leverage will press the ball carrier to the outside support players and to the sideline, thus limiting the field of play.

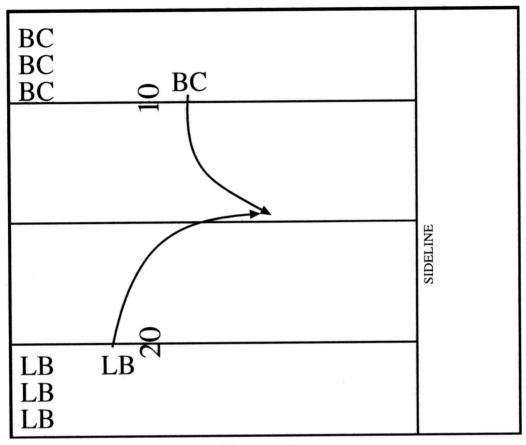

Diagram 3.4
The showdown is an open-field tackling drill.

➠ The defender should focus eyes through the hips of the ball carrier to eliminate the possibility of the defender going for a fake move.

➠ The defender should close on the ball carrier with controlled speed. If the tackler should stop his feet, the ball carrier will undoubtedly be successful. Even if the tackler is running but without controlled speed, it will be difficult for him to react to any cuts the ball carrier may make.

➠ Very seldom will an open-field tackle be a pad-under-pad hit. The tackler should make the hit with an outside-shoulder hit to eliminate the ball carrier's inside cut. The tackler should then finish the tackle by pressing the ball carrier off the sideline or getting two fists full of cloth.

➠ This drill is conducted at full speed, with the initial hit being live. However, the tackler should not take the ball carrier to the ground. Once the tackler has secured the ball carrier with both of his hands or the ball carrier has crossed the end line, the coach should whistle to end the play. A potential for injury exists during this drill if the coach lets the tackler go after the ball carrier's ankles or if he lets it turn into a wrestling match. This exercise is a great drill to film for teaching players. As a rule, this drill can be done once or twice a week.

➡ The ball carrier and the tackler start the drill 5-10 yards apart. As players show improvement, the distance can be widened. The tackler aligns on the top of the field numbers, while the ball carrier aligns on the bottom of the field numbers **(DIAGRAM 3.4).**

➡ The ball carrier runs anywhere from the bottom of the numbers to the sideline. The ball carrier's objective is to get past the tackler.

➡ The ball carrier can go any time after the coach gives a voice command to begin the drill.

CONVERGE TACKLE DRILL

The purpose of this drill is to develop a linebacker's open-field tackling skills when converging on a ball carrier with another tackler. The primary emphasis of the drill is to develop awareness of the other tackler's positioning on the ball carrier **(DIAGRAM 3.5).**

➡ This drill is a full-speed tackling exercise up to the point of contact with the ball carrier. Coaches need to be very quick on their whistle to stop the drill. It can be a relatively dangerous drill if the tacklers are not controlled.

➡ Two tacklers are aligned 10 yards away from each other on a line. The ball carrier aligns 10 yards from the two tacklers, splitting the distance between the two tacklers **(DIAGRAM 3.5).**

➡ On the coach's "READY" command, the ball carrier can run anywhere in the 10-yard box to get past the tacklers.

➡ The tacklers perform full speed until contact takes place.

Key Coaching Points
The tacklers develop the skill of leverage awareness on a ball carrier. The tacklers should overplay their near side to insure that the ball carrier will not escape. The tackler should force the ball carrier to the tackler's partner.

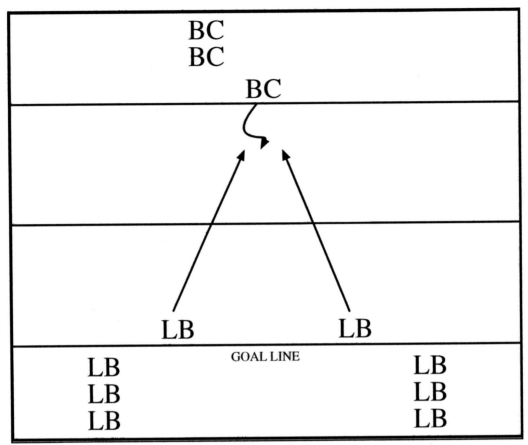

Diagram 3.5
Converge tackle drill.

➡ The tacklers should close on the ball carrier with controlled speed, while maintaining outside leverage. The defenders should always close ground on the ball carrier.

➡ The tacklers should verbally communicate if they are inside or outside the ball carrier. The tacklers should know that they are in a converge-tackle situation.

➡ Unlike a one-on-one tackle, the tacklers should not try to work their helmet across the front of the ball carrier because they would lose their leverage positioning.

➡ The tacklers should focus their eyes through the hips of the ball carrier to eliminate the possibility of going for a fake move.

➡ The tacklers should squeeze cloth with their hands to finish the hit

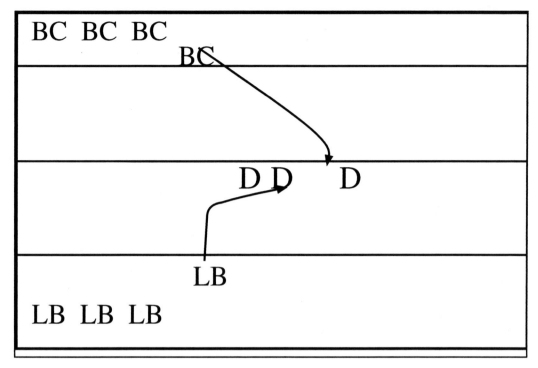

Diagram 3.6
The tight-to-green drill teaches the linebacker to eliminate the cutback run.

➡ The tacklers should drive their feet through on contact and push the ball carrier back where he started.

COMING TIGHT TO GREEN DRILL
This drill is designed to develop the skills and ability of linebackers to attack the line of scrimmage on a path that keeps them close to the inside edge of the hole. We call this "coming tight to green." The linebacker to the front side of a play is responsible for the hole in the direction the ball carrier is running. The ball carrier often sees and attacks the same hole. It is vital that the linebacker does not overrun the hole or scrape to the outside edge of the hole. If the linebacker scrapes to the outside edge of the hole, he loses his inside-out leverage on the ball, and he comes into the ball carrier's vision early enough for the ball carrier to make a cut off the linebacker. The drill involves the following steps:

➡ The linebacker is positioned 10 yards from the ball carrier. Three players are aligned shoulder-to-shoulder, with blocking dummies next to each other, left or right of the ball **(DIAGRAM 3.6).**

➡ On the coach's command, the ball carrier should run at 90% speed to a hole that presents itself. Prior to the snap, the coach signals which dummy holders will slide to develop a hole. Two of the three dummy holders slide to develop the hole on the snap.

➡ The linebacker attacks the hole, maintaining inside leverage on the ball carrier, and scrapes as tightly as possible to the inside edge of the lineman in the hole.

➡ The linebacker should not take the ball carrier to the ground.

Key Coaching Points

Engaging in the drill enables the tackler to develop the skill of "coming tight to green." The drill also allows the defenders to develop a feel for how a hole may change during a particular play during the game. Points of emphasis for each defender include:

➡ Close on the ball carrier with controlled speed.

➡ Keep his toes pointed towards the line of scrimmage so that he has a good power base to make the tackle and any opportunity for hidden yardage is strictly limited.

➡ Focus his eyes through the top of the ball carrier's thigh pads in order to enhance his ability to react to movement of the ball carrier.

➡ Make a pad-under-pad hit on the ball carrier. Hitting with leverage can enable him to overcome a lot of potentially serious tackling mistakes.

➡ Cock and shoot his hands up on contact. This action is designed to get his hips involved in the hit. Players should be constantly reminded that their hips are the most powerful part of the human body. As such, once their hips are involved, less chance exists for hidden yardage.

➡ Squeeze cloth with his hands to finish the hit.

➡ Drive his feet through on contact and push the ball carrier back where he started.

➡ Put his helmet across the ball carrier's sternum to insure that his tackle does not turn into an arm tackle.

CHAPTER 4

OPEN FIELD TACKLING (OFT)

Open field tackling (OFT) is very different than any other form of tackling. Even though many of the base, form-tackling principles discussed earlier in this book are applied to OFT, this type of tackling is extremely unique. We believe this type of tackle is the most challenging and, accordingly, needs to be drilled every day. In addition, we stress to the rest of the defense that this skill is one of the toughest to master in football. This factor helps to explain why effective pursuit is so important.

The question arises regarding when this type of tackling is used. We teach our players to use this technique any time the ball carrier has either separation or distance from the defensive back or a perimeter position. While many types of open-field tackles exist, each of which are discussed in this chapter, all open-field tackles have a set of seven common principles.

SEVEN BASE PRINCIPLES TO OPEN-FIELD TACKLING:

1) *Know where your help is.* This principle is the most important of the seven. For a corner in a deep 1/3, all 10 teammates will be to the inside (**Diagram 4.1**). Obviously, the corner does not want the ball carrier to go outside. A key coaching point is to keep the ball carrier inside in front of the tackler. As such, the perimeter defenders should be taught to always make inside-shoulder tackles (except the sideline and cutback tackles). We use this same concept on our punt-coverage and kickoff-coverage teams, as well. Pursuit from the rest of the defense plays a huge role in helping our perimeter players. We want our corners to be confident that they will get help to the inside.

2) *Close the gap.* The defender needs to close the gap on the ball carrier, or take away ground as quickly as possible. We teach our defenders to close to four yards. This will cut the angle down for the ball carrier and make it easier for the defender to mirror the ball carrier. If the defender sits back and waits, the ball carrier will have room to make moves. Both concepts are illustrated in **Diagram 4.2**.

3) *Come under control and keep the feet active.* After closing the gap to four yards, the defender must come under control. He should be taught to "buzz" the feet or "throttle" down and continue to inch toward the ball carrier. In order to react in the

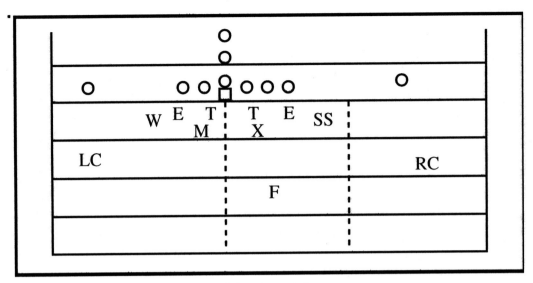

Diagram 4.1

The right corner's help is inside. He has 10 teammates inside him. We want him to make an inside-shoulder tackle.

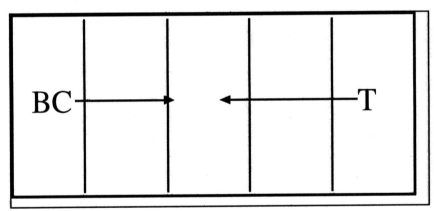

Diagram 4.2
Close the gap.

open field, tacklers must shorten their stride and come under control. If the defender is out of control, it will be easy for the ball carrier to make him miss. The tackler MUST NOT stop his feet. This is why we teach inching forward. If the defender stops his feet, he will not be able to react quickly to the ball carrier. In addition, a key coaching point is to have the tackler take the stagger out of his feet once he has closed the gap (**Diagram 4.3**). This action will make the tackler throttle down. The defender must keep his toes parallel to the ball carrier. If they are staggered, the tackler will cross his feet and be more likely to miss tackles.

4) *Lower the center of gravity*. This action must occur when the tackler "throttles" down. An easy way to teach a defender to lower his body weight or center of gravity is to have him put his arms down to his side. This is a basic defensive back principle when coming out of a back pedal and breaking on the ball. To go from backward to forward, we teach players to shorten their stride and lower their arms. These two tips will help players keep their feet under their shoulders and lower their center of gravity, allowing for quicker reactions.

5) *Eyes on the hips*. We put black Velcro patches just above the thigh boards to train the tackler where to look. Some coaches teach players to concentrate on the bottom of the numbers. We think this landmark actually moves, allowing the tackler's eyes to drift upwards. Focusing on the hips trains the tackler what to look for when the ball carrier makes cuts.

6) *Mirror the ball carrier*. The OFT does not have to be pretty. Rarely will an OFT be a great form tackle. If the techniques discussed previously have been employed, it will be relatively easy for the defender to react efficiently. Ideally, the defender should stay in front, with a slight outside shade as long as possible. In this regard, the tackler should be a "basketball defender". Mirroring the ball carrier means mirroring with the feet, hips and shoulders. If the ball carrier makes more than one move, pursuit should help in the tackle. With his toes parallel to the ball carrier, his body under control and his feet buzzing, the defender should step with the foot in the direction of the cut (**Diagram 4.4**). Open-field tacklers should never cross their feet to mirror the ball carrier. Once this foot action occurs, the tackler's hips and shoulders no longer mirror the ball carrier. Furthermore, the defender will not be able to react in the other direction.

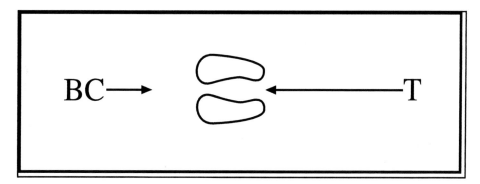

Diagram 4.3
The tackler should take the stagger out of his stance and bring his feet parallel on approach.

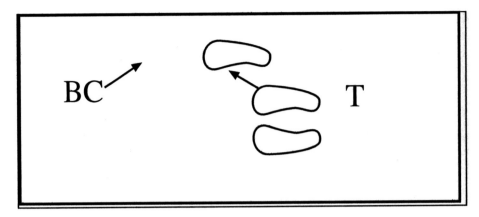

Diagram 4.4
The tackler steps with his right foot to mirror the ball carrier.

7) *Wrap up/grab cloth.* When the defender mirrors the ball carrier, he has an arm length to both sides to make a tackle, as seen in **Photo 4.1**. In other words, the tackler has one-arm length of error to each side. We do not want to arm tackle in the open field, yet we still want to emphasize moving the feet. However, there are so many different open-field scenarios that sometimes, we are content to just get the ball carrier down. We <u>DO NOT</u> teach tackling low in the open field. This approach typically causes the head to go down and may result in an injury and many more missed tackles. We want the tackler to envelop the ball carrier with the his arms around the ball carrier's upper body. We have had defensive backs that remind us of octopuses, they wrap every tentacle around the ball carrier. Grabbing cloth in all tackles should be stressed. In Chapter 2, the importance of building forearm strength by executing towel pull-ups in the weight room discussed. This exercise has helped our player's grip strength tremendously and cut down on the number of missed tackles in the open field.

OPEN FIELD TACKLING DRILLS

OFT BETWEEN THE LINES
Diagram 4.5 illustrates this drill. The focus of this drill is to develop a proper concentration point of the eyes, while keeping the feet active and mirroring the ball carrier. This drill is a physical and mental warm-up before going into other OFT drills. Since this drill is close quartered, it is the first one we teach. This exercise is a great concentration drill since the ball carrier will make an abnormal number of moves or jukes. During the drill, we repeatedly command "feet, feet, feet; eyes, eyes, eyes." We do this drill everyday.

Photo 4.1

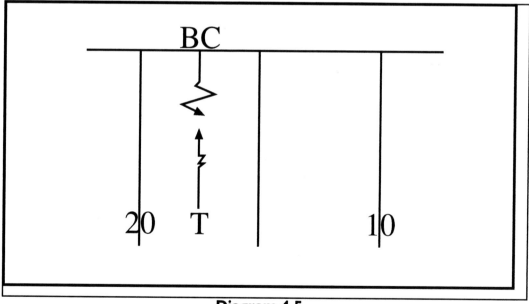

Diagram 4.5
OFT between the lines drill.

Setting up the drill:

➡ The ball carrier will start on the sideline, while the tackler will start on the bottom of the numbers (seven yards from the sideline).

➡ The ball carrier must stay between the lines. His goal is to make it to the numbers.

➡ On command, the ball carrier can make as many moves as he wishes.

➡ The tackler should close ground and then throttle down, staying in front of the ball carrier while keeping his feet active.

➡ This exercise is a full-speed drill. We want a live wrap up. However, both the ball carrier and the tackler should stay on their feet.

15 YARD OFT

Diagram 4.6 illustrates this drill. This drill addresses all seven principles of open-field tackling. After the OFT between the lines drill, we go directly to this drill. Because this drill operates in a larger open space, it is more realistic for the defensive back. As with the OFT between the lines drill, this drill should be performed every day. Again, during the drill, the command, "feet, feet, feet; eyes, eyes, eyes," is continuously repeated.

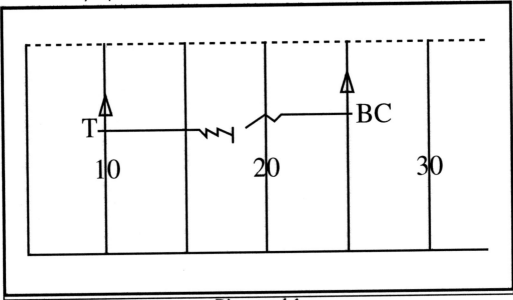

Diagram 4.6
15-yard open field tackle.

Setting up the drill:

➥ The defender should always be told where his help is. The tackler should start just outside the ball carrier.

➥ Cones should be used to designate where the tackler and ball carrier start. Cones help control the spacing of the drill. As tacklers become more skilled, the area in which the drill is conducted can be widened.

➥ On command, the ball carrier and the tackler start forward. The ball carrier is allowed no more than two moves.

➥ The keys for the tackler are: close as much ground as quickly as possible, come to a control position slightly outside the ball carrier, keep his feet buzzing and parallel, mirror the ball carrier, and grab cloth.

➥ Common errors: players don't come under control and don't keep their feet under themselves; players cross their feet; tacklers lunge; and tacklers don't keep the ball carrier inside and in front of them.

➥ This exercise is a full-speed drill. We want a live wrap up. However, both the ball carrier and the tackler should stay on their feet.

COMPETITION OFT
This is a variation of the two previous drills. However, the resultant combination adds fun and competition to the drill. **Diagram 4.7** illustrates this drill.

Setting up the drill:

➥ The group is divided into tacklers and ball carriers, 25 yards apart.

➥ The hash mark is used as one out-of-bounds line, while a set of cones–15 yards away– is positioned as the other out-of-bounds line. As the tacklers become skilled at the drill, the space employed in the drill between the line of cones and the hash mark can be increased.

➥ This drill can be conducted at two tempos. One can be like the other drills: live wrap up, with the ball carrier and the tackler staying on their feet. The other tempo could be live to the ground. Because of the risk of injury, we will not allow tacklers to grab ankles. The coach should use a quick whistle if the defenders start involving the ball carrier's ankles in their tackling efforts.

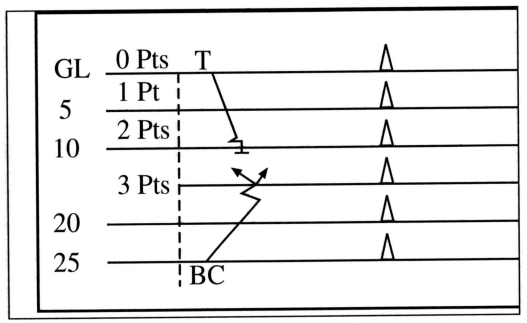

Diagram 4.7
Competition OFT.

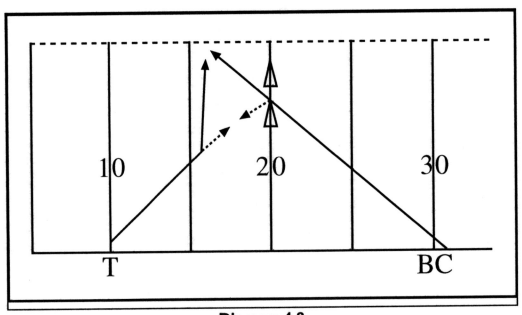

Diagram 4.8
Chute tackle.

➡ This drill is a competitive exercise, designed to reward tackles made as close to the line of scrimmage as possible. Any tackle made between the 10-yard line and the 25-yard line is worth three points. Tackles made between the 5-and the 10-yard line are worth two points. A tackle made between the 5-yard line and the goal line is worth one point. If the ball carrier crosses the goalline, no points are awarded to the tackler.

➡ The coach determines the number of points. If the tempo is live to the ground, it is fairly easy to determine points. If the tempo is live on the feet, then the tackler must be in control of the ball carrier.

➡ Each tackler should keep track of his own points. The first tackler to reach 10 points is declared the winner.

CHUTE OFT

Diagram 4.8 illustrates this drill. This drill teaches the tackler what to look for when a ball carrier is making his cut. Two things typically happen when a ball carrier makes a cut: 1) he shortens his stride length; and 2) he lowers his off hand. This drill is designed for a defensive back that suddenly has a ball carrier shooting through the line of scrimmage. The ball carrier does not have time for a lot of moves since he is close to defenders. We do this drill once per week.

Setting up the drill:

➡ The ball carrier is on the sideline at the 30-yard line.

➡ The defender starts on the sideline at the 10-yard line.

➡ A gate of cones are set up between the numbers and the hash mark at the 20-yard line.

➡ The ball carrier is instructed to go through the gate of cones and either cutback or keep running at the same angle. No juking or slow-and-go is allowed. The ball carrier either cuts back or keeps running the same speed.

➡ Verbal cues should be given to the tackler during the drill: e.q. , "eyes," "keep your feet under yourself," "stay square," "stay inside – out, etc."

CUTBACK OFT

Diagram 4.9 displays this unique drill. This drill is tailored for the backside defensive corner, who is in pursuit of a ball carrier who has broken through the first and second levels of defense. The defensive back suddenly finds himself on an island. We developed this drill after giving up a couple of long touchdowns in this situation. The mistakes the corners made were similar to a commonly missed tackle in the open field. We decided to make this drill specific to the situation and instruct the defensive backs to use their open-field tackle techniques and pursuit rules.

Setting up the drill:

➡ The ball carrier is positioned on the hash mark, five yards from the goal line. The corner starts at the 10-yard line, between the opposite hash and the numbers. Another DB is located to the inside so that the corner and ball carrier know where the pursuit is. Cones are used in the drill, as shown.

➡ On the coach's command, the DB backpedals. At the same time, the ball carrier jogs to the first set of cones.

➡ When the ball carrier gets to the first set of cones, the coach yells "run, run, run." The corner should immediately break and start pursuing the ball carrier. Having reached the first set of cones, the ball carrier can start to run at full speed through the second set of cones.

➡ The ball carrier is allowed to make one move. If he makes more than one move, pursuit will tackle him. The ball carrier should be instructed to make one move and then get up the field!

➡ The corner should remember the following pursuit rule: keep the ball inside and in front. He should remember, that all of the his help is to the inside. In addition, we want the corner to be in front of the ball with a slight outside shade. If the corner does not get in front, the ball carrier will run right past the converging defensive backs.

➡ The corner should sprint to a spot to close ground. We call this spot the junction point. Once he has closed ground on the ball carrier, he should square up his shoulders and get his feet under himself, protecting the edge.

➡ The common mistake of the corner is that he does not square up and come under control. This mistake can allow the ball carrier to simply make one move and get outside.

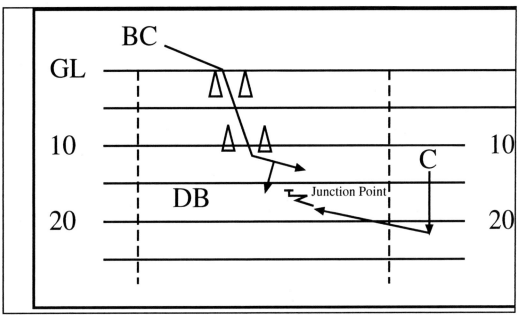

Diagram 4.9
Cutback OFT.

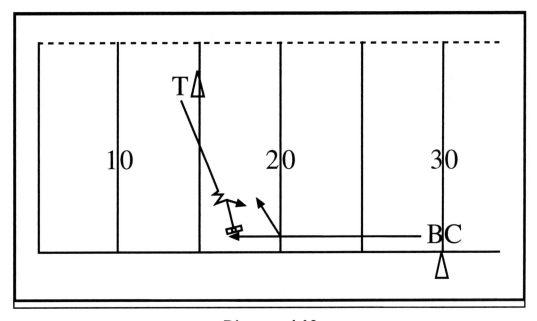

Diagram 4.10
Sideline tackle.

➠ Having reached the junction point, all the OFT techniques now apply.

➠ This exercise is a unique drill that has saved us at least one to two touchdowns per year. This specific situation does not occur often, maybe once every two games. Accordingly, we feel it is important enough to conduct the drill once every 2 - 3 weeks. The main point of the drill is to enable the corner to know what to do in this situation.

SIDELINE OFT

Diagram 4.10 illustrates another unique drill that was developed after our defense gave up several long touchdown runs. As in the "cutback OFT" drill, this drill is designed for a pursuing defensive back. The drill involves a scenario where a ball carrier is sprinting down the sideline with a defender pursuing from the inside. A unique feature of this drill is that the tackler will make an outside-shoulder tackle. We want to use the sideline and pin the ball carrier with the tackler's outside shoulder. If the tackler tries to make an inside-shoulder tackle, the ball carrier can make a "stop and go" move, causing the tackler go past him. This mistake "opens the gate" that often will enable the ball carrier to score. On the other hand, the tackler does not want to ball carrier to simply beat him down the sideline. This drill involves an extremely difficult skill and takes considerable practice for the tackler to be able to judge where he should throttle down. We execute this drill once per week.

Setting up the drill:

➠ A cone is positioned 15 yards from the sideline and 15 yards from the ball carrier. This point is where the tackler will start.

➠ Another cone is placed on the sideline, 15 yards from the tackler.

➠ On the coach's command, the ball carrier begins sprinting down the sideline, and the tackler begins to converge on the ball carrier.

➠ The ball carrier should be convinced of the fact that he has one defender to beat for a touchdown. At the tackler/ball carrier-junction point, the ball carrier can do one of three things: 1) sprint down the sideline; 2) use a "stop and go" move and shove the tackler past if the tackler overshoots him; or 3) he can use a cutback move.

➠ The pursuing tackler should sprint to a spot to close ground. We call this the junction point. Once he has closed ground on the ball carrier, he should square up his shoulders and get his feet under himself. At this point, the tackler must react to the ball carrier.

➡ The tackler should be instructed to key the inside number of the ball carrier. If it disappears, the ball carrier is going down the sideline, and there will be no cutback. The tackler should use an outside-shoulder tackle so that he does not overshoot the ball carrier. This instance is one of the few times the tackler's helmet will be behind the ball carrier.

➡ If the tackler can still see the inside number of the ball carrier, he should anticipate cutback. The defender should use the sideline and squeeze the runner out-of-bounds.

3-STEP OFT

This drill is specifically for off-corners. An off-corner is defined as a defensive corner who is 7-8 yards off the receiver to his side. He is responsible for a deep-zone or man coverage. The purpose of this drill is to combine the skills involved with defending the 3-step pass with a corresponding open-field tackle. Whether in a man or zone coverage, we defense the 3-step pass in the following way:

➡ The off-corner walks out of his backpedal. If he bursts out at the snap, he won't be able to break effectively on the ball.

➡ As the corner walks out of his backpedal, he keys the QB. He wants to determine if the play is a 3-step pass or not.

➡ If the play is a 3-step pass, he immediately breaks and goes to the receiver. He must secure the up-field shoulder of the receiver before looking back to the ball.

➡ If the play is not a 3-step pass, the corner backpedals quickly for depth and plays the run or the deep route. Even though the speed of the backpedal has changed, we still want the corner to be under control. If the corner needs to go full speed, he should turn and run.

Setting up the drill:

➡ The ball is placed either on the hash mark or the middle of the field. To maximize repetitions, the players are divided into two groups–a boundary group and a field group. Each group consists of a corner, a QB, and a receiver. After each repetition, the players rotate positions (responsibilities).

➠ The offense determines the receiver's route, while the other side executes the drill. For the 3-step routes, the offense can run a 5-yard hitch, a 5-yard out or a 5-yard slant. To keep the corner playing honestly, the offense can run a go (or fade) route and a post route. We also mix in the hitch-and-go route and the out-and-up route.

➠ When the corner recognizes the 3-step drop of the QB, he immediately breaks to the receiver and executes an OFT. We want a live wrap up. However, both the ball carrier and the tackler should stay on their feet.

➠ A run scheme can also can be incorporated into the drill to make the exercise more realistic. For example, the QB can run down the line, and the receiver can stalk or crack block. The corner must now react to a number of situations, rather than just playing the 3-step game. It makes the drill more "game-like." We conduct this drill twice per week.

Hips OFT

The purpose of this drill is to teach players to get their hips in front of the ball carrier after contact is made on an angle tackle. A ball carrier will often continue to gain yardage since his momentum is going forward. To offset the ball carrier's momentum, tacklers should not continue on their same angle of contact. They must get their hips around in front of the ball carrier and drive him backwards.

Setting up the drill:

➠ Similar to the angle tackle in the Progression, players are paired up on a line. One group is designated as a tackling side, while the other side acts as the ball carriers. Each group is positioned three yards apart. The players should spread out. With no pads, the tackler and the ball carrier should be an arms length away from each other. With pads on, the tackler and the ball carrier can be up to three yards apart. The tackler and the ball carrier should be positioned at a slight angle to each other. The coach should specify the direction of the ball carrier and the tackler.

➠ On the "ready" command, the tackler gets into a bent-knee position with his arms ripped back at 90 degrees. On the "hit" command, the ball carrier will run at a 45-degree angle. The tackler will explode his hands through the ball carrier and will drive the ball carrier backwards.

CHAPTER 5

TAKEAWAY

Attempting to take the ball away from the offense is a fundamental part of every tackle. We coach it on every snap during practices and games. Every snap of the ball is an opportunity for the defense to take the ball away from the offense.

We use the term "takeaway," rather than "turnover." We want our players to understand that the offense does not turn the ball over to us; rather, we take it away from them. A coach should develop a relentless takeaway state of mind in his players by emphasizing takeaways through drills in practice, talking about takeaways in team meetings, and having a designated staff member as the takeaway coach.

The takeaway coach is the most important element in developing the relentless takeaway mind set in the players. In any scrimmage setting in practice, the takeaway coach will call out repeatedly "get the ball out" or "take the ball away" on every snap. The players will hear this call to action on every snap and start to become very conscious of stripping the ball. We find our players are yelling "get the ball out" while the play is in progress in practices and games. The takeaway coach can still coach his position. In addition, a team's offense will benefit by learning to take better care of the ball when the offense is scrimmaging against a takeaway – minded defensive unit.

It takes time for the defense to develop the relentless , takeaway state of mind. Seasoned defenders will pick it up more quickly because they have mastered their fundamental skills and responsibilities. Because unseasoned players often have too much on their minds, taking the ball away is either overlooked or not given a priority status.

Stripping the ball properly involves adherence to specific techniques and fundamentals. As such, it is important that some kind of takeaway drill is conducted in every practice. Drilling will greatly increase a team's takeaway productivity. In that regard, we have observed a noticeable drop in the number of takeaways when we have not drilled it enough in practices. The players must understand that making the tackle is the highest priority. The first defensive player to the ball carrier should make the tackle, while the second and third defenders should attempt to strip the ball. The only time the first defender to the ball carrier should attempt to strip the ball is when the tackler is in a trail position. These situations will be addressed in further detail in the following sections.

STRIPPING THE BALL

We teach four methods of separating the ball from the ball carrier. The first was addressed in the earlier sections of this book. We emphasize the explosive extension of the tackler's hips by teaching a double upper cut with the tackler's arms. The tackler's hips are the key to aggressive hits that can cause the ball carrier to lose control of the ball. The other three techniques are: 1) the secure-and-punch-under technique when trailing the ball carrier; 2) the secure-and-punch-over-the-top technique when trailing the ball carrier; and 3) the lift-and-tear technique when the ball carrier is already secured by another tackler.

Tackling and stripping when behind the ball carrier
We teach two methods of stripping the ball from behind, based on what the ball carrier is giving the tackler. If the ball carrier has a high hold on the ball , brown from the ball will be showing under his arm (**Photo 5.1**). In this scenario , the tackler will use the punch-under technique. If the ball carrier has a low hold on the ball , then the brown of the ball shows over the top of his arm (**Photo 5.2**). In this case, the tackler should strip the ball by punching over the top. Rule: Punch where there is the most brown of the ball showing.

1. Secure-and-Punch-Under Technique
➠ The first part of the secure-and-punch-under technique is to secure the tackle. When tackling and stripping the ball carrier from behind, it is important that the tackle is secured. It is easy for the tackler to get too greedy and not secure the tackle.

➠ The tackler secures the ball carrier by shooting his arm over the shoulder of the ball carrier and grabbing the ball carrier's shoulder-pad breast plate (**Photo 5.3**).

➠ With his hand nearest to the ball , the tackler should punch under the ball from behind with an upper cut (**Photo 5.4**).

➠ When the ball is separated from the ball carrier , the tackler must still maintain control of the ball carrier so that the ball carrier does not recover the ball. As noted in the pursuit section, we want all 10 of the other players pursuing to the ball so that the probability of our taking the ball away is increased.

Photo 5.1

Photo 5.2

Photo 5.3

Photo 5.4

Photo 5.5

➠ We prefer the punch-under technique in comparison to the punch -over technique. The ball carrier is taught to hold the ball on three points: the eagle claw of the hand on the point of the ball; the arm on the body of the ball; and the body of the ball on the ribs of the ball carrier. The punch -under technique is more effective because it pushes the ball away from the ball carrier's ribs where he is attempting to secure the ball. The punch-over-the-top technique is not as effective in forcing the ball away from one of the three points the ball carrier uses to secure the ball.

➠ Setting up the drill: The players are divided into pairs. They then alternate securing the ball and performing the punch-under technique from a standing trail position.

2. Secure-and-Punch-Over-the-Top Technique

➠ The first part of the secure-and-punch-over-the-top technique is to secure the tackle. When tackling and stripping the ball carrier from behind, it is important that the tackle is secured. It is easy for the tackler to get too greedy and not secure the tackle.

➠ The tackler should secure the ball carrier by shooting his arm over the shoulder of the ball carrier and grabbing the ball carrier's shoulder-pad breast plate (**Photo 5.3**).

➠ With his hand nearest to the ball, the tackler should punch the ball over the top of the ball carrier's arm (**Photo 5.5**).

➠ Setting up the drill: The players are paired up. They then alternate securing the ball and performing the punching-over-the-top technique from a standing trail position.

➠ The trail strip drill , discussed in the next section, is an effective exercise for teaching these skills.

TRAIL STRIP DRILL

The purpose of this drill is for players to learn how to recognize where to punch the ball and to learn the proper techniques for stripping the ball from the ball carrier when tackling from a trail position. This drill schould be done once a week for at least five minutes.

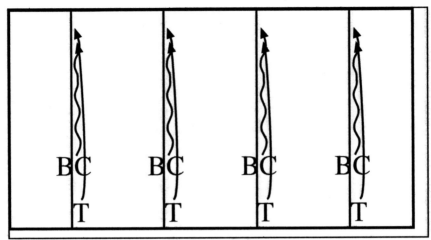

Diagram 5.1
The trail strip drill is an effective way for players to get many repetitions in a short time.

➠ The players are divided into pairs and positioned on a line facing the same direction. The pairs are spread out on the field (at least five yards apart) to lessen the likelihood of collisions (**Diagram 5.1**).

➠ Acting as a ball carrier, the lead player has a ball tucked under his arm. He should put only 75% pressure on the ball. If he squeezes the ball too tightly, the drill can turn into a wrestling match.

➠ The other player, serving as the tackler, assumes a trail position behind the ball carrier.

➠ On the coach's command, the ball carrier gets into a slow run, and the tackler begins to close on the ball carrier from behind. It is important to keep in mind that this closing is not a race.

➠ The coach can predetermine the type of strip the tackler will concentrate on (e.q. , secure-and-punch-over either from the top or from underneath). If working the punch-under technique, the ball carrier has a high hold on the ball and is showing the ball under his arm. If working the punch-over-the-top technique, the ball carrier has a low hold on the ball, and the ball is showing over the top of his arm. The coach does not have to predetermine the technique, and the ball carrier can change up how he holds the ball.

➡ The players continue taking turns stripping the ball and changing the sides on which they are working.

➡ The coach should keep the player's focus on the task at hand. Because several balls are rolling around, there is opportunity for the players to get distracted. Once the drill has been performed, the coach should get them back into pairs as soon as possible and start another repetition of the drill.

➡ As many repetitions of the drill as possible should be completed as quickly as possible.

3. Lift and Tear Technique

➡ The lift-and-tear technique is used when a tackler secures the ball carrier, and a second defender has his hands on the ball. This exercise is the most often used technique for stripping the ball from the ball carrier.

➡ The second defender lifts the elbow of the ball carrier to separate the ball from the carrier's ribs (**Photo 5.6**).

➡ With his opposite hand, the second defender grabs the point of the ball nearest to the ball carrier's elbow and attempts to tear the ball out **(Photo 5.7)**

➡ The players are divided into pairs. One player serves as a ball carrier, while the other acts as the tackler. Alternately, they practice lifting the elbow and tearing out the ball.

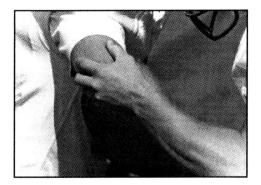

Photo 5.6

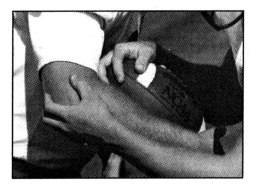

Photo 5.7

DIAMOND TACKLE DRILL

This drill is designed to serve two key purposes: 1) to develop the skills of a good form-angle tackle on the ball carrier; and 2) to develop the lift-and-tear technique by the second defender. This exercise is a live drill that should be practiced at least once a week.

➠ The ball carrier aligns himself five yards from the tackler. The coach stands 1-3 yards to the left or right of the tackler. The second defender lines up five yards behind the coach (**Diagram 5.2**).

➠ Any time after the coach's "ready" call, the ball carrier runs directly at the coach. This action keeps the ball carrier from flattening his path to avoid a hard hit. The closer the coach is to the tackler, the tighter the angle of intersection and the higher the impact on collision. The coach can lessen the intensity level of the collision on impact by widening his alignment from the tackler.

➠ On the ball carrier's movement, the tackler accelerates through the ball carrier with a proper technique hit, driving the ball carrier back. The ball carrier should not be taken to the ground. (Refer to the tackling progression chapter for a more extensive discussion of the steps involved in angle tackling).

➠ The second defender accelerates to the ball carrier. On arrival, the second defender lifts the elbow of the ball carrier and with his opposite hand tears the ball out by grabbing the point of the football opposite of the ball carrier's hand.

➠ After the ball has been stripped, the tackler should keep the ball wrapped so the offense cannot regain possession of the ball.

➠ The second defender then scoops up the ball and accelerates for five yards towards the end zone. The technique for scooping and recovering the football is addressed in the next section.

➠ As many repetitions of the drill should be completed as quickly as possible.

TRIANGLE STRIP DRILL

This drill is designed to serve two key purposes: 1) it develops strip skills in a gang-tackle situation; and 2) it develops a tackler's skill of making the tackle, while letting the other players take the ball away from the ball carrier. This drill places less physical impact on the tackler and the ball carrier than the diamond tackle drill.

➠ Three tacklers line up 1-2 yards from each other in a triangle set. The ball carrier aligns three yards from the tacklers (**Diagram 5.3**).

➠ The coach should organize as many 4-player groups as feasible to maximize the time available and get the most repetitions possible.

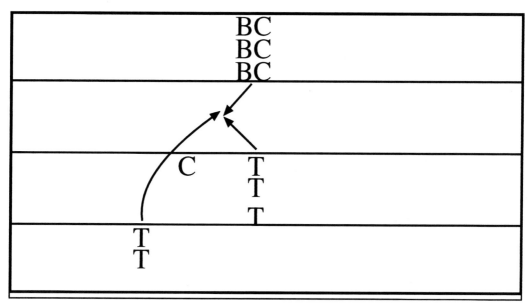

Diagram 5.2
The diamond tackle/strip drill gets the players to tackle and strip the ball.

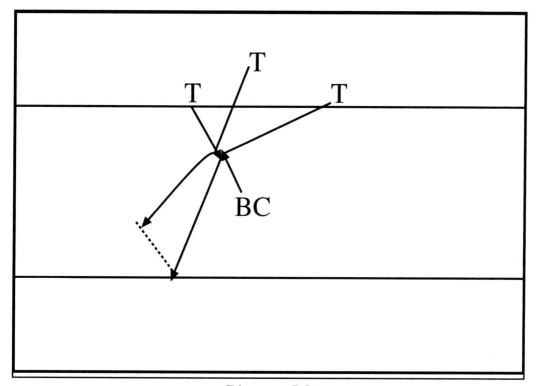

Diagram 5.3
The triangle strip drill puts the players in a gang-tackle situation.

➠ Anytime after the coach's "ready" call, the ball carrier runs at the first or the third tackler.

➠ The tackler makes a proper technique hit and drives the ball carrier back. The ball carrier should not be taken to the ground.

➠ The remaining defenders strip the ball.

➠ The tackler should maintain control of the ball carrier so that he is not able to recover the ball.

➠ After the ball is stripped, the remaining defenders scoop the ball and execute a pitch.

RECOVERING THE FOOTBALL

We teach two methods of recovering a football on the ground: 1) covering and 2) scooping. We encourage our defensive players to attempt to score whenever they have opportunity. We want them to scoop the ball when they recognize that there are no opposing players near the ball. If the player doubts that he can scoop the ball successfully, then he should cover the ball.

Scooping the football

➠ If players have any doubt that they can scoop the ball successfully, then they should cover the ball.

➠ When scooping a football on the ground, players should keep their poise. When the ball is on ground, a player should accelerate to the football and come to a stop over the ball. Often, players panic and try to run at the same time they are scooping.

➠ When he is over the ball, the defender should bend at the knees, ankles, and hips to scoop the ball, rather then bending over at the waist and keeping his knees locked **(Photo 5.8)**. This approach will prevent a situation where the player kicks the ball he is trying to scoop.

➠ It should be emphasized to the players that they should use two hands to pick up the football. Sometimes players get sloppy by using one hand if the coach does not keep reminding them of the proper technique.

Photo 5.8

➡ Once the football has been secured, the defender should lock it away. We teach our players three points of contact on the football: 1) the hand eagle-clawed on the point of the ball; 2) the forearm on the football; and 3) the body of the ball pressed into the player's ribs. The ball carrier should get both hands on the ball when coming into contact with a tackler.

➡ We allow our players to pitch the ball to a teammate when they have only one threat, and they are confident that they can complete the pitch.

Covering the football

➡ When covering the football, it is important that the player hook slides into the ball. A player's body should cup around the ball so that it will not squirt away (**Photo 5.9**).

➡ Players should not be allowed to roll over the ball when they are coming into the ball, because such an action will give the opposition an opportunity to take the ball back.

Photo 5.9

Photo 5.10

➠ When covering the ball, the player should get as much of his body around the ball as possible–arms, torso, legs and knees on the ball. The player who recovers the ball should not let the ball see daylight. (**Photo 5.10**).

➠ Players should not jump on top of a ball on the ground because the ball could squirt out if another player jumps on the cover player. Also, players who jump on top of a ball are putting themselves in a position to possibly get injured if another player should land on them.

➠ When the ball is covered, the recovering player's teammates should cover him to protect him from the opposition taking the ball from him in the pile.

INTERCEPTING A PASS

Among the key points for developing the skills involved in intercepting a pass is the need to make time for players to catch footballs during practice. Our players play catch with each other before practice. It is fun for the players, and it does not take time out of practice. Another method we use to develop our defenders' pass-catching skills is to have them catch a plastic football on an elastic cord. The practice helps them develop hand/eye coordination, and they can get numerous repetitions in a relatively short period of time. Other key concepts in intercepting a football include:

➠ The defender should always comeback to the ball when the ball is in the air. He should attack the ball just as the receiver would do. The defensive player must become a receiver. He should run to the ball and jump up for the ball. He should catch the ball at the highest point possible and as close to the line of scrimmage as possible, in order to lessen the opportunity for the receiver to step in front of the defender and catch the ball.

➠ When catching the football, the defender should extend his hands out to the ball. His eyes should look the ball into his hands when his hands and arms are extended. If his hands are close to his body, the player's head needs to move to look the ball into his hands. Because nobody can consistently react as quickly as necessary, this lack of needed reaction time in every situation and is often the reason why a player does not catch balls consistently.

➠ A defender should catch a high pass with his thumbs and pointing fingers together, his arms extended, and his eyes looking through the opening between his pointing fingers and thumbs (**Photo 5.11**).

➡ A defender should catch a low pass with his littler fingertips together and extended away from his body (**Photo 5.12**).

➡ Once the football has been secured, the defender should then lock it away. We teach our players three points of contact on the football: 1) the hand eagle-clawed on the point of the ball; 2) the forearm pressing on the football; and 3) the body of the ball being pressed into the player's ribs. Accordingly, a ball carrier should get both hands on the ball when coming into contact with a tackler.

➡ After catching the football, the defender should take the ball up the nearest sideline. He should put the ball in the arm closest to the sideline. The other defenders will be better positioned to block. After intercepting the pass, the defender should not run the ball into the middle of the field where the offense typically has most of its players.

➡ The second player to arrive at the interception should block the receiver. After an interception, most tackles are made by the intended receiver.

➡ On recognition of an interception, the defensive linemen are responsible to block the quarterback. The quarterback is often the last line of defense the offense has in preventing an interception being run back for a touchdown by the defense.

TAKEWAY CIRCUIT

The takeaway circuit is comprised of three drills that emphasize takeaway fundamentals. A coach should divide his defense into three equal groups. The players practice at each station for two minutes. The drills should be performed at least once a week.

COVER AND SCOOP THE FOOTBALL DRILL

This drill is designed to develop the skills involved in covering or scooping a football on the ground. These techniques were addressed in detail in the first part of this chapter.

➡ The players align in two parallel, single-file lines facing the coaches. The coaches are five yards from the front of the lines (**Diagram 5.4**).

➡ One line works on scooping the football, while the other line is involved in covering the football.

Photo 5.11

Photo 5.12

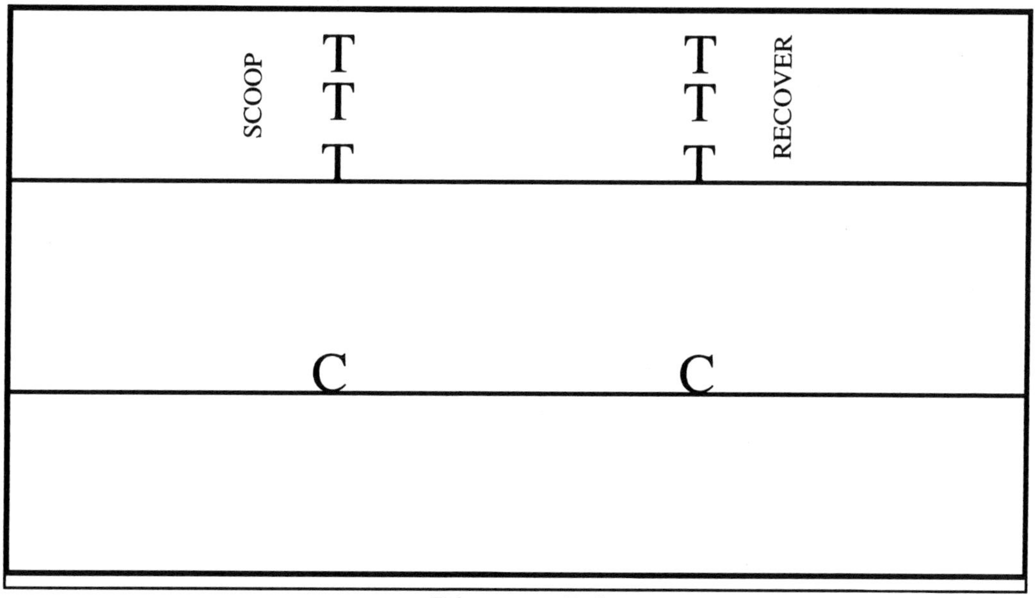

SCOOP T T T T T T RECOVER

C C

Diagram 5.4

The cover and scoop the football drill allows the players to perform multiple repetitions.

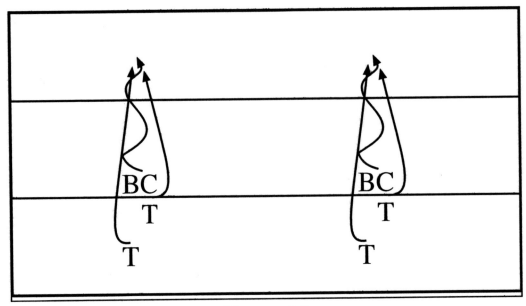

Diagram 5.5

The train strip drill is designed to work defenders in a trailing strip position on a tackle.

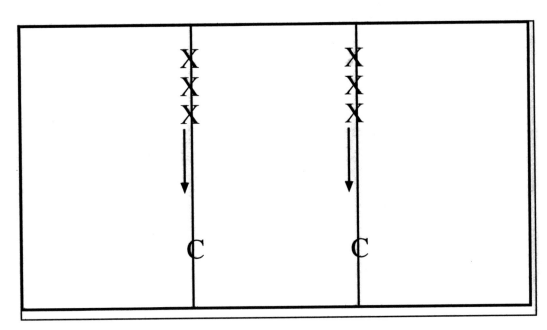

Diagram 5.6

Down the line interception drill.

➦ The players rotate between the lines so that they all get practice at both techniques.

➦ On the coach's command, the players in the front of the line rapidly fire their feet in place. The coach points left or right, and the players react and open their hips in the direction the coach is pointing. this action is called quarter-eagle turns. The coach then rolls the ball on the ground, and the players execute their designated recovery technique.

➦ Each coach should have 3-4 balls for the drill. Once the ball is recovered, the players should set the ball next to the coach.

➦ As many repetitions of the drill as possible should be completed as quickly as possible.

TRAIN DRILL

This drill is designed to develop the skills involved in taking away the football when the defender is in a trail position. In addition, this drill helps develop the skills involved in executing a lift-and-tear technique to take away the ball when the defender is the second player to arrive at the tackle. These techniques were addressed in detail in the first part of this chapter.

➦ The players match up in groups of three.

➦ Only two groups will perform the drill at a time.

➦ On the coach's command, the ball carrier starts running at 2/3 speed, with the tackler trailing (**Diagram 5.5**).

➦ The tackler attempts to strip the ball by executing a secure-and-punch-under or secure-and-punch- over-the-top technique.

➦ The second defensive player executes a lift-and-tear technique if the tackler did not strip the ball.

➦ If the tackler strips the ball, the second defender executes a scoop technique to recover the ball on the ground. The tackler should maintain possession of the ball carrier to lessen the possibility that the ball carrier will recover the football.

➦ As many repetitions of the drill as possible should be completed as quickly as possible.

DOWN THE LINE INTERCEPTION DRILL

This drill is designed to develop the basic skills involved in catching (intercepting) a high or low pass. These techniques were addressed in detail in the first part of this chapter.

➡ The players align in two single-file lines (**Diagram 5.6**).

➡ Two coaches assume a position ten yards from the first player in each of their lines.

➡ On the coach's command, the first player in a line runs at the coach in front of his line.

➡ The coach throws the football, and the player catches the ball.

➡ The coach can throw the ball to the player at eye level or at waist high. On the high pass, the ball should be caught with the end of a player's thumbs together; on the low pass, the ball should be caught with the end of the player's little fingers together.

➡ The coaches will need 2-3 balls each to keep the drill moving quickly. A player should stand next to each coach and feed him balls to help increase the number of repetitions that are performed.

➡ As many repetitions of the drill should be completed as quickly as possible.

OTHER RELATED DRILLS

QUARTERBACK BACKSIDE HIT AND STRIP DRILL

This drill is designed to reinforce the proper techniques involved in tackling a quarterback and to practice stripping the ball when the quarterback does not see the rusher coming. This drill should be done a minimum of once every two weeks

➡ A quarterback is positioned at a 7-yard depth from the line of scrimmage (**Diagram 5.7**).

➡ On the snap of a football, the pass rusher works a pass-rush move on a pass protector. The pass protector lets the pass rusher win by not giving too much resistance. It should be kept in mind that this exercise is a tackling drill, not a pass-rush technique drill.

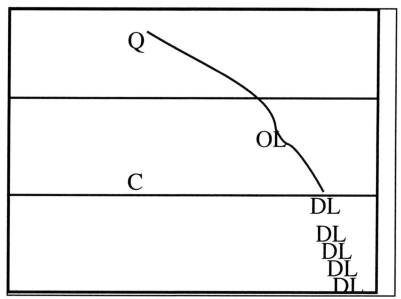

Diagram 5.7
Quarterback Backside Hit/Strip Drill

➠ It is still essential that the pass rusher executes a crisp pass-rush move to lessen the opportunity for developing bad habits.

➠ It is important that the pass rusher accelerates to the quarterback after defeating the pass protector's block.

➠ On impact with the quarterback, the pass rusher should take his arm nearest to the line of scrimmage and secure the tackle. The tackler should let up slightly before contact and not take the quarterback to the ground in the drill. The other arm should spike at the football in an attempt to get it out of the quarterback's grasp.

READING PITCH OR KEEP DRILL
This drill is designed to develop the skills involved in making a lateral pitch after making a scoop recovery. This drill should be performed no more than once every weeks.

➠ A line of defenders aligns five yards from the coach (**Diagram 5.8**).

➠ A second line of defenders aligns five yards behind the first line of defenders.

➠ On the coach's command, the ball is rolled on the ground.

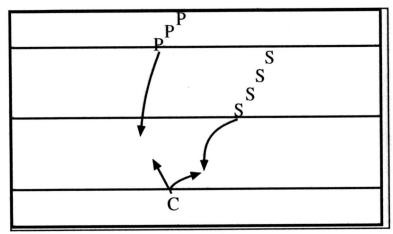

Diagram 5.8
The pitch the ball drill teaches the players to be smart with the ball.

➠ The defender executes the scoop technique to recover the football. (The steps for performing a scoop technique properly were addressed in an earlier section).

➠ The trail defender communicates to the scoop player that they are in the pitch phase. The trail defender stays behind and outside the scoop player, so that the read player cannot make a play on both players.

➠ The coach takes the role of being the tackler of either the scoop player or the pitch player. The scoop player reads the tackler to determine whether to pitch or keep the ball.

➠ The scoop player should understand that although we want to score as a defense, he must not pitch the ball unless he is 100% sure that the pitch will be completed successfully. It should be strongly emphasized that we do not want to give the ball back to the offense by making a poor decision on the pitch.

➠ To enhance the level of the player's motivation any time we put the ball on the ground during the drill, the players owe ten push-ups at the end of the drill. On the other hand, the coach owes the players twenty push-ups if there is only one football on the ground during the drill.

CHAPTER 6

PURSUIT

Why is pursuit the most important skill to be taught?

➡ Pursuit will make a poorly talented defense good, an average-talented defense very good, and a very-talented defense great.

➡ Pursuit can make up for the failure of a player to properly execute his assignment or for a missed tackle.

➡ Pursuit is a major key in taking the ball away from the offense. When the ball is on the ground, the more people the defense has near the ball, the higher the probability the defense will recover the football.

The key objective in teaching pursuit is to ensure that every player understands that every snap of the ball in practice and in a game should involve 100% effort. Accordingly, every player should sprint to the ball at full speed until the whistle is sounded. Anything less then 100% effort is considered a lack of commitment to the team. Team players give 100% every snap. It is critical that all coaches understand that pursuit effort is the most important skill that is taught and evaluated every snap. It is easy as a coach to get so caught up coaching his position that he forgets to coach pursuit effort.

When we grade our game film, the players are evaluated on their pursuit effort. If a player is recognized as a jogger on film, he must address the entire defense at the Sunday-night meeting. At that time, the defensive coordinator will announce to the team that there was a jogger in the game. Then, the player will step forward and address the entire team. The defensive players and coaches will be on one knee. The jogger will stand in front of the team and say " I jogged yesterday. I am sorry for letting the team and myself down. It will never happen again." The players and coaches will stand, and on the jogger's command, everybody executes one up/down on the ground. The offending jogger will then bring the defense together, and the team will break on his command. Having the jogger break the team out brings him back into the fold of the team. Although the exercise is designed to embarrass the jogger because of his actions, at the end of the exercise, the team brings him back into the unit. Very seldom will a player repeat as a jogger. We have had only one player repeat as a jogger in six years.

PURSUIT DRILL

This drill is designed to develop the skills involved in executing proper pursuit angles. This drill should be practiced once every two weeks. It should be noted that the key to developing proper pursuit is coaching and placing an emphasis on executing proper pursuit on every snap during practice. Although helpful in this regard, performing the Pursuit drill is secondary in importance.

Key Coaching Points

➡ A defender should never follow the same colored jersey. When following a team-mate, there is one less defensive player that can make a play.

➡ The corner to the side of an outside-run play should serve as secondary-run support and should stay outside and in front of the ball.

➡ The corner away from the side of a run play should follow the "21" rule. The corner keeps all 21 of the other football players inside and in front. This action will keep the backside corner in a position to make a play if the ball carrier cuts back or continues downfield.

➡ Typically, the defensive end, the defensive tackle, and the outside linebacker away from the play need to take drastic angles of pursuit to cross in front of the ball carrier's path. If the ball carrier has excellent speed, and the defender's speed is not comparable, the defenders may need to aim their path of pursuit near the goal line.

➡ It is best for a defender to overestimate his angle of pursuit because it is easier to readjust his angle by bending it back.

The offense consists of a quarterback, the defensive coordinator, two running backs, and two wide receivers (**Diagram 6.2**). The offense can execute four different plays: toss sweep, option, boot pass, and reverse. (**Diagrams 6.2, 6.3, 6.4, 6.5**). The coordinator numbers the plays and signals to the offensive players what play they should execute. When conducting the drill, the following points apply:

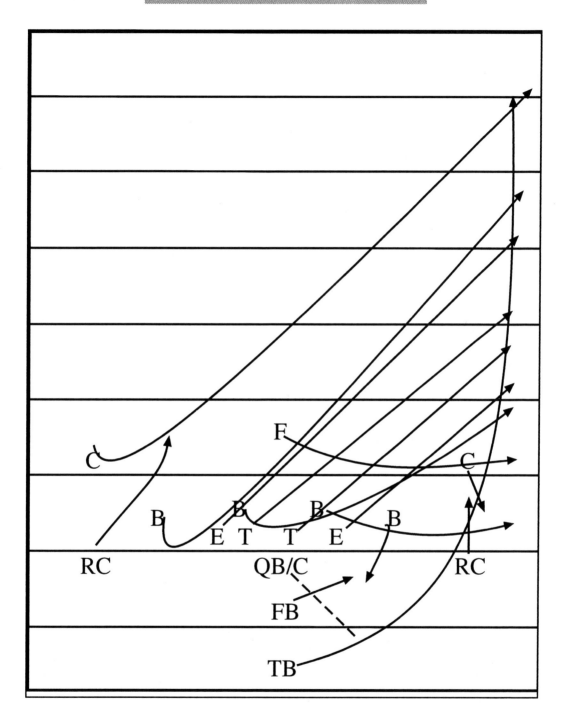

Diagram 6.2
Toss sweep pursuit drill.

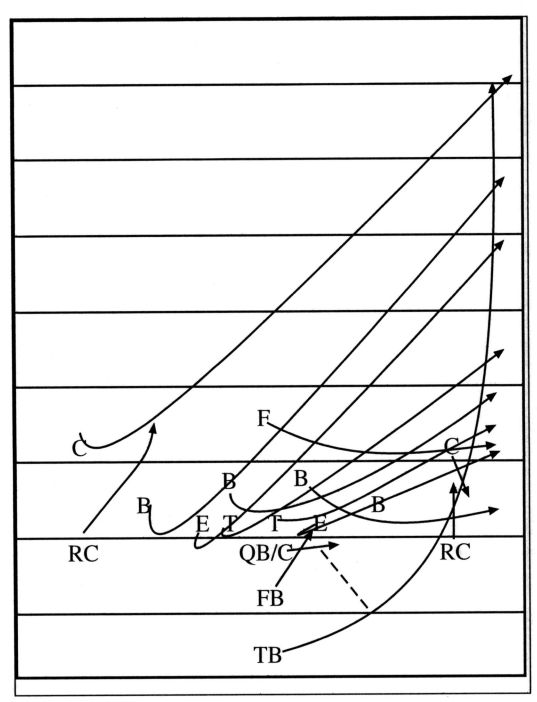

Diagram 6.3
Option pursuit drill.

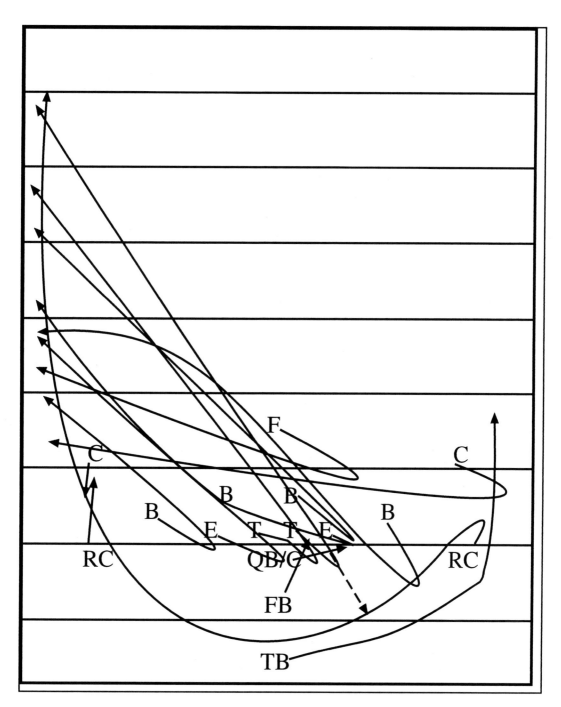

Diagram 6.4
Reverse pursuit drill.

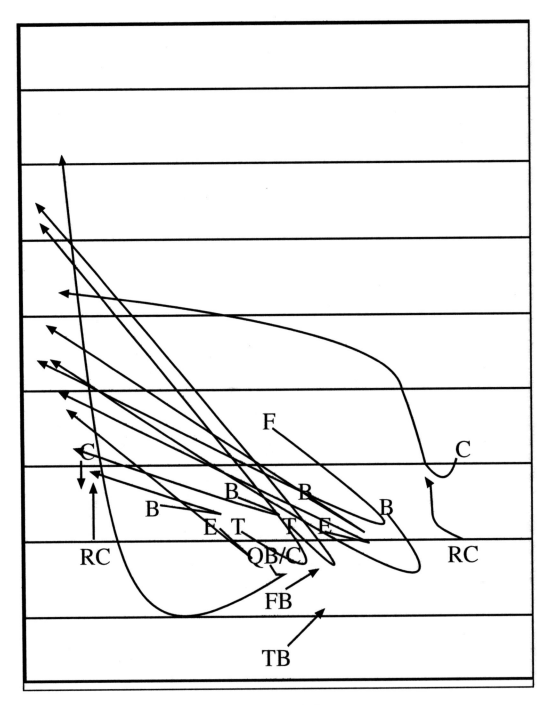

Diagram 6.5
Quarterback boot pursuit drill.

➠ The entire defense should align in their base defensive call. On the snap of the ball, the defense should execute an up/down, hit their chest to the ground, and bounce back to their feet.

➠ The defensive players should pursue at angles that will enable them to cross in front of the ball carrier. If any player cannot pursue and cross in front of the ball carrier, that group is required to repeat the drill until every player crosses the ball carrier's path.

➠ After a player crosses in front of the ball carrier's path, he turns facing toward the field in a power football position, rapidly firing his feet in place. Once every defensive player has crossed the ball carrier's path, the players then run back to their starting point together.

➠ It should be emphasized that *nobody* should touch the ball carrier. If the ball carrier is hindered, the drill is too easy.

CHAPTER 7

SUMMARY POINTS

When we were approached to write a book and help produce an instructional video series, the first topic we thought of was tackling. Then after we had taken the opportunity to review the literature on tackling, we were amazed at the lack of published information on the subject available.

The following points summarize what has been discussed:

➡ The following base elements of tackling were examined in detail in this book:
   ✔ Tackling
   ✔ Taking the ball away from the offense
   ✔ Pursuit

➡ As coaches, we put a high premium on coaching tackling, pursuit, and taking the ball away in every individual, group and team period.

➡ Tackling is the most important and fundamental skill in playing defense.

➡ Safe and proper tackling involves adherence to specific fundamentals and techniques.

➡ The proper body position and contact points when executing a safe tackle are reflected in the phrase "the four ups of tackling": head up, eyes up, chest up, and arms up.

➡ Filming tackling drills is invaluable. We film all of our tackling drills for evaluation and for teaching. Players need to see proper tackling techniques, as well as have the opportunity to address incorrect tackling technique.

➡ The tackle progression or circuit tackling is the keystone of how we teach tackling. Among the advantages of the Circuit are the following:
   ✔ It involves a high number of repetitions without high-speed impact. As a result, the Circuit is an exceptionally safe way to get hundreds of reps.

     ✔ It can be implemented without pads.

     ✔ Players learn what to do with their arms when tackling.

     ✔ High reps with low impacts allows everyone to experience success; subsequently, this success can have a positive impact on the players' confidence level.

     ✔ Players who have initially been shy of contact learn to accept contact and turn out to be solid tacklers.

     ✔ Players get to know and feel proper contact points.

     ✔ Players know what to do with their feet on contact.

➠ Regardless of position, we believe in tackling everyday.

➠ Position-specific drills (discussed in Chapters 2 though 4) can serve as an invaluable resource for a team's coaches.

➠ Stripping the ball from a ball carrier is a fundamental part of tackling.

➠ Teaching players to take the ball away from the ball carrier and how to re-cover the ball can involve a variety of techniques that should be taught and emphasized during pre-season workouts and re-emphasized throughout the season.

➠ Taking the ball away from the offense should be a fundamental part of every tackle. We coach it on every snap during practices and games. Every snap of the ball is an opportunity for the defense to take the ball away from the offense.

➠ Pursuit can enable the defense to overcome most mistakes.

➠ Pursuit can make a poorly talented defense good, an average-talented de-fense very good, and a very-talented defense great.

➠ Pursuit is a major key in taking the ball away from the offense. When the ball is on the ground, the more people the defense has near the ball, the higher the probability the defense will recover the football.

The very fact that you are reading this book indicates you are one of those individu-als who has a strong desire to constantly improve your teaching techniques. In addi-tion, you are the type of coach who is always looking for ways to put your players in the best position to succeed. The most effective way we know to improve a defense is to improve tackling fundamentals and techniques.

If the material in this book helps you in your endeavor to develop a successful football program, then the effort to write it will have been worthwhile.

Kevin Bullis is the defensive coordinator at the University of Wisconsin—River Falls. Prior to accepting his present position in 1995, he served as the defensive coordinator for Gustavus Adolphus College for two seasons. He is a graduate of the University of Minnesota—Morris, where he played football for four seasons and earned all-conference honors in 1987. Kevin and his wife, Cathy, have two sons—Jack and Joe.

Tom Journell is the assistant head football coach at the University of Wisconsin—River Falls. Prior to joining the Falcons' staff in 1989, he was on the football staff at Miami of Ohio. A graduate of Wittenburg University (Ohio) where he played both football and baseball for four years, he also serves as the strength and conditioning coach for all UW—River Falls athletic teams. Tom and his wife, Betsy, have one son—Mack.